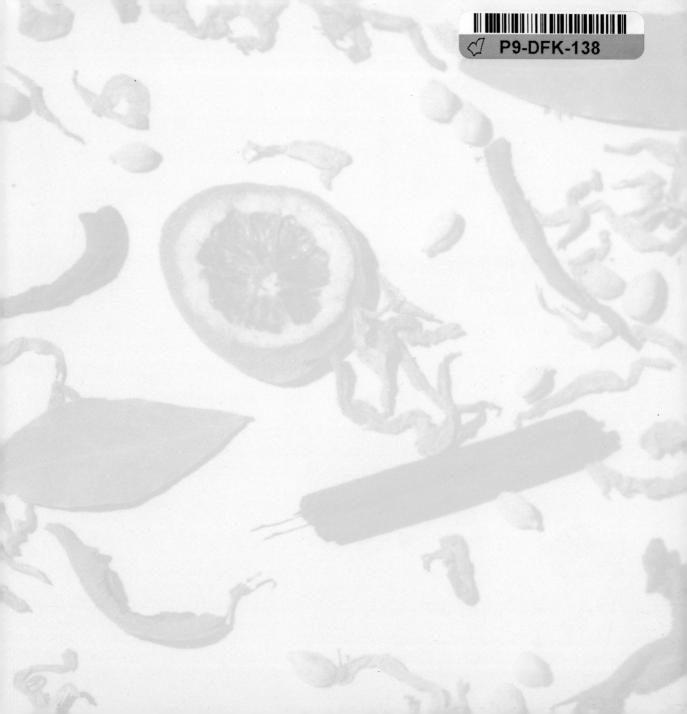

GIFTS
FROM THE HERB
GARDEN

GIFTS
FROM THE HERB
GARDEN

emelie tolley

& chris mead

Designed by Susan Slover Design

CLARKSON POTTER/PUBLISHERS

NEW YORK

To my family and friends. CM
To Sarah, Andrew, and Toby Ann
with love. ET

Published by Clarkson N. Potter, Inc., 201 East 50th Street, New York, New York
10022. Member of the Crown Publishing Group.

CLARKSON N. POTTER, POTTER, and colophon
are trademarks of Clarkson N. Potter, Inc.

Manufactured in Japan

Library of Congress Cataloging-in-Publication Data

Tolley, Emelie.
    Gifts from the herb garden / Emelie Tolley and Chris Mead.—1st ed.
        p.   cm.
    1. Herbs—Utilization.   2. Flower arrangement.   3. Nature craft.
    4. Holiday decorations.   I. Mead, Chris, 1959–   .   II. Title.
    SB449.3.H47T65   1991
    635'.7—dc20

91-11729
CIP

ISBN 0-517-57562-0
10 9 8 7 6 5 4

So many people we have met since we
started working on our first book, *Herbs,* almost ten years ago have contributed to *Gifts from the
Herb Garden.* We thank them all for sharing their knowledge
and enthusiasm, especially: Kenneth Turner who inspired us from
the beginning; Betsy Williams; Polly Haynes; Audrey Julian; Carol
Pflumm; Helene Koch; Haskell's Nursery; Quail Mountain Herb Farm;
VSF; Nancy Lindemeyer and *Victoria* magazine; Allen Schneider; Elizabeth
and Patrick Gerschel; Patti Kenner; and Susan Clapp. A special thanks to
Betsy Yastrzemski whose help in creating wreaths and arrangements
was invaluable and to Susan Slover Design for their skill in combining
modern design with a traditional subject to create a beautiful
book. And, of course, our ongoing appreciation to Pam
Krauss, a devoted editor, and to all our friends at
Potter whose encouragement, help, and
knowledge made it all
possible.

HERBAL SCENTS

HERBS FOR THE HOLIDAYS

SWAGS & GARLANDS

HERBAL BEAUTY

Mounds of heady lavender and pungent thyme, graceful stalks of silvery artemisia, a rampaging clump of pot marjoram covered with purple blossoms, deliciously scented full-blown roses—there is nothing more beautiful or more rewarding than an herb garden. When you walk through such a garden you are constantly amazed by the endless variety of textures, colors, and scents; the smallest thyme blossoms demand as much admiration as a stately foxglove; and

A generous bunch of lavender, this from Meadowsweet Herb Farm, tied with a pretty ribbon, is the simplest way to add this fresh scent to your home: place it on a living room table, stash it in a drawer, or tuck it into a linen closet.

the sensual fragrances of delicate rose-scented geraniums, spicy pinks, or citrusy mints perfume the air. Working among these pleasing plants doubles the joy of gardening for even the most passionate gardener, and there's no greater pleasure for an enthusiastic cook than surveying a garden full of tasty herbs while deliberating over which flavor will enhance the evening's menu most or which flower will make the platter most appealing. It's hard to leave so much beauty outside, so both cook and gardener soon seek ways to bring the rewards of the garden indoors. It may be nothing more than a little herbal bouquet sitting on the kitchen windowsill to please the eye while providing inspiration for culinary talents, or a more ambitious bouquet with the added dimension of fragrant greenery and delicate herbal flowers.

As summer goes on, you begin to think about drying your harvest so you can enjoy the color and fragrance of the garden through the long days of winter. What exquisite pleasure to meander among the plants on a clear summer's day, searching for a flower or a bunch of soft gray lamb's ears or mugwort at the peak of perfection. As you fill your basket with the herbs you've selected to dry, visions of dried bouquets, wreaths of every size and shape, fragrant potpourris and sachets, imaginative topiaries, even

simple natural beauty creams and lotions tease your imagination.

The possibilities of herbs are unlimited, and by combining herbs with flowers and vegetables from the garden, those possibilities are broadened even further. Somehow these fragrant plants seem to call forth unique creative talents, especially in herb crafting. Whether you simply tie a bunch of lavender with a pretty ribbon, create the lushest,

VSF's moss-covered pot rimmed with colorful flowers.

Lavender lines a flower-decorated moss basket from VSF.

most elegant garland to adorn your mantel, or blend a jar of fragrant bath herbs, these simple plants can add a warm and gracious note throughout the house. In this book you will find exciting variations and unexpected approaches to everything from potpourris and topiaries to Christmas decorations and bath products. We hope looking through it will stir your creativity. The photographs will spark ideas for unusual

containers, such as a pitcher for a topiary or a shell for potpourri, suggest new uses for common materials —garlic turned into a handsome kitchen topiary, for example—and encourage you to discover ways of using the creations from your garden in every room in your home.

If you do not have a garden, or if your garden can't produce everything you need, you will find suppliers of dried materials in the source

Blackrock Farm's tussie-mussie recalls a summer garden.

list at the back of the book. And for those whose time is short or who are unsure of their talents, we offer a directory of others who make and sell glorious wreaths and topiaries, potpourris, and natural cosmetics.

Whether you make them yourself or partake of someone else's creativity, we hope this book will inspire you to enjoy the gifts of the garden more than ever before.

What could be prettier—or more fragrant—than this rose-lined garden trug. To make one yourself, cover the inside of a trug with moss.

Coat the inside of the basket with white glue or spray glue and press on dried rose petals. Affix bunches of roses, wheat, salvia, white yarrow, and other herbs and

flowers around the rim with a hot-glue gun. Use the same technique for the moss pots, far left and center.

Dried herbs and flowers make it possible to enjoy the beauty of the garden year round. They impart their warm color and subtle fragrance to everything from herbal decorations and potpourris to cosmetic vinegars and topiaries, so it's worth taking a little time during the summer to dry your favorites as they reach perfection in the garden. When fall comes, you will have a wonderful selection of rich yellows, gentle grays, intense blues, lovely pinks, pretty purples, and a myriad of greens, shapes from spiky to round, and textures from velvety soft to crisp and crinkly to inspire you to create handsome wreaths or bouquets, sweet-smelling sachets, or soaps to remind you of the pleasures of a summer garden.

1

To be dried successfully, herbs and flowers must be picked at their peak. For foliage such as the artemisias, this often means before the flowers bloom. Flowers should be open but not too full blown. Avoid any plant that has begun to turn yellow or brown. For the greatest fragrance and endurance, it is best to gather your herbs before the heat of the day has had time to disperse the oils or cause the plants to wilt. If possible, wait until the morning dew has had a chance to evaporate and the plants are dry. Be sure to pick more material than you think you need since it will shrink as it dries, and inevitably some will not dry to perfection.

Very Special Flowers sets a miniature wreath of apple mint and oregano on a moss-covered Styrofoam base around a candle, *left*. An obelisk from Afton Grove, *right*, made of Sty-rofoam, cut to shape and glued together, then covered with various types of moss.

AIR DRYING

Air drying is the simplest method and works for most herbs and flowers, although you may find that flowers' color fades somewhat if they are beyond their prime and the humidity in the atmosphere is high. Gather smallish bunches of herbs and tie them together at the bottom of the stem with string or raffia. Make sure the string is very tight, as the stems will shrink as they dry. (You can also secure the stems with a rubber band, which will contract as the stems shrink.) Hang the bunches upside down from a drying rack, a ceiling beam, pegs, or even a hanger in a dry, airy spot out of direct sunlight. They will be dry in anywhere from a few days to two weeks or more depending on the thickness and moisture content of the leaves, stems, and flowers and

the amount of humidity in the air. For example, a thin-leafed plant such as mint will dry more quickly than silver king artemisia. Although leaves are traditionally stripped from flower stems before drying, I have

found this unnecessary if the plant does not have a high moisture content. Roses, for example, dry beautifully with the leaves intact. The herbs and flowers are dry when the leaves and petals are crisp to the touch.

Individual large leaves such as angelica, rose, or other petals for pot-pourri, and single flowers heads should be air-dried by spreading them out in a single layer on a screen or other surface that will allow air to circulate around them easily. When dry, store in airtight jars.

DRYING MEDIUMS

Silica gel or other drying mixtures such as clean sand or a mixture of two parts cornmeal to one part borax are especially good for drying flowers when maintaining the shape and color are important. Although silica gel is relatively expensive, it can be reused indefinitely and works extremely well. Be careful when using it, however, as it is unhealthy to inhale the fine dust that fills the air when you pour it. Either wear a nose mask or ladle the gel gently from one container to another.

Place a 1-inch layer of the drying mixture on the bottom of a shallow box, then carefully arrange the flower heads on top: upside down for single-petaled flowers such as pinks, right side up for more complex flowers such as roses. Gently spoon more of the drying medium around and over the flowers, being careful not to distort their shape. To dry roses and other fairly thin-stemmed flowers on their stems complete with leaves, lay them in a layer of silica gel on their sides in a large box. Cover with more gel, then close the box tightly and set it aside. Check to see if the flowers are dry after two days for thin-petaled flowers such as pansies or pinks, longer if the flowers are full petaled. When they are completely dry, they will be crisp and paperlike to the touch. It is important to check frequently, however, since if the flowers are left in too long, they will become brittle and very fragile. Remove the flowers from the drying mixture very carefully. If any

Opposite: A bower of dried flowers hanging from old English clothes drying racks. Although Flowers Forever's straight-forward geomet-ric arrangement of roses, statice, wheat, tansy, and lavender, *above,* is simple, it has great style. It re-quires patience to insert the stems with such careful precision; marking the design on the Oasis base serves as a guideline.

In her flower-filled workshed, Emelie Tolley works on dried arrangements, potpourris, and other herbal delights. Flowers hang from the ceiling on old English clothes drying racks and on wall racks rescued from an old tobacco shed. Shorter stemmed varieties are heaped in baskets. Cabinets hold dried herbs for potpourris and cosmetics.

Tropaeolum majus

You can use pressed and dried herbs and flowers to make decorative prints, cards, or even bookmarks. To make a decorative herbal print, press herb leaves and flowers between sheets of blotting paper or newsprint in a flower press or heavy book until crisp and dry, then affix in a pleasing arrangement with white glue.

petals are dislodged as you take them out, simply reattach them with a spot of white glue. Gently shake out any extra mixture, and if necessary, use a small paint brush to whisk away stubborn bits. Store the dried flowers in a tightly covered box with a small amount of silica gel until you are ready to use them. To prevent the dried flowers from reabsorbing the moisture in the air, spray them with hair spray or a special florist's protective spray before using them in arrangements.

Whole flower heads can be glued to wreaths, topiaries, or whatever project you are working on. To use them in dried arrangements, insert a piece of florist's wire through the center of the head, make a small hook in the wire on the top side of the flower, then pull it back down until it catches in the flower. The wire stem should then be wrapped in green florist's tape before it is used in the arrangement.

You can speed drying time considerably by "cooking" flowers in silica gel in a microwave oven, but there are drawbacks to this method. Since most microwaves are relatively small, you can dry only a small amount at one time. It also requires a great deal of experimentation to find the correct times and temperatures for various plants, and the process does not work well with flowers that contain a great amount of moisture: they tend to turn brown. If you would like to know more about microwave drying, there are books devoted solely to this subject.

An American Indian birch basket is a handsome container for Flowers Forever's precise arrangement of poppy heads.

DEHYDRATION

Dehydrators combine heat and circulating air to dry very efficiently. Although they are available with various numbers of trays so you can dry a fair amount at one time, the lack of space between the trays can limit their usefulness. They are extremely helpful, however, for quickly drying fruit such as apple and orange slices, small flowers, sprigs of herbs such as thyme, and single leaves and petals. The temperature and length of time best suited to each item can be determined from reading the instruction book that comes with your dehydrator and through experimentation.

FREEZE DRYING

Freeze drying is the newest method for preserving everything from leeks to roses. The machines are expensive to purchase and to run and, therefore, not practical for home use. These costs are reflected in the price of freeze-dried products, although to have mushrooms, carrots, herbs, and flowers that last indefinitely and look as if they had just been pulled from the garden makes the prices palatable for special projects.

Freeze-dried roses are quite readily available through flower markets and by mail, and now there are small independent suppliers across the country who sell a wider range of freeze-dried items or who will work to order on anything from a special flower to a tussie-mussie. See the directory for sources of freeze-dried herbs, flowers, and vegetables.

Flowers Forever's market basket filled with freeze-dried vegetables, *below,* would be a handsome addition to any kitchen year round, bringing with it memories of visits to your favorite farm stand. An old tole and brass container, *opposite,* holds an arrangement of yellow and white yarrow, poppy heads, safflower, wild marjoram and lavender.

TO

A dark green forest of miniature myrtles clustered in a window; two stately bays guarding a front door; a fragrant feathery lemon geranium tree scenting a bathroom: herbal topiaries add visual charm anywhere they are placed. When Roman gardeners created the art of trimming trees and bushes into fanciful shapes in their ornamental gardens, they couldn't have guessed they were launching a gardening style that would endure thousands of years. During the Renaissance, when men

Preceding page:
Afton Grove's moss-covered cone with garlands of cranberries, lady apples, millet, tallow berries, yarrow, and rose hips. The special charm of Afton Grove's topiary, *right,* comes from the proportions and the subtle colorations and differing textures of wild marjoram, thyme, thistles, artemisia, and white yarrow. A lush fresh rose topiary, *opposite,* growing from an antique porcelain container is lovely for a special occasion. Carve an oval or **sphere out of one or two pieces of Oasis, then wrap the shape in chicken wire. Dampen the Oasis and set it on a dowel covered with moss and dried rose petals. Insert short-stemmed roses directly into the damp Oasis as close together as possible, and fill any gaps with rose leaves. Keep the Oasis damp and your topiary should last for several days.**

gloried in controlling nature, no garden worthy of the name was without sculptured hedges. Green animals, birds, and even elaborate topiary tree houses grew in imposing gardens. By the eighteenth century, however, the fashion had changed; gardens that imitated and improved on nature were the rage and topiaries became an oddity. They never totally disappeared, though, and over the years a few industrious gardeners have devoted themselves to preserving this garden artform. Today their whimsical shapes and elegant contours are once again delighting garden lovers.

Until a few years ago most of us never considered having a topiary of our own. Then some inspired soul began training small herb plants into the appealing little lollipop trees known as standards. Now fragrant spheres of rosemary, delicately airy balls of curry plant, and dense, dark green orbs of myrtle are among the most popular of all herbal decorations. Although these little round trees have a special naive charm, triple balls, cones, and rings can be

equally pleasing. Their architectural shapes work well in formal or informal rooms, and if you haven't the right conditions for a living topiary, one of dried materials is a splendid substitute. While one tree is fine, a pair of lavenders flanking a doorway or setting off a mantel is even better, four little rose trees marching down the center of a dining table make a superb centerpiece, and a collection of graduated myrtle plants set out on a large table, mixed perhaps with a collection of garden ornaments, is absolutely enchanting. And what a wonderful present a ring of pungent rosemary abloom with tiny blue flowers or a big ball of lemon geranium dotted with delicate pink blossoms would be.

live topiaries

Growing a live herb topiary requires time and patience. If you choose a slow-growing plant such as myrtle or rosemary, it may take two or three years before you have anything resembling the little trees you see at the florist. Moreover, the standard will not be particularly pretty or

decorative during the growing period. If you are impatient, perhaps you would be smarter to go to the local nursery or order your little tree by mail. However, the sense of accomplishment derived from creating your own topiary will more than repay your efforts, and if you want a very special shape or an unusual herb, you may have no choice but to undertake the project yourself.

Before you start, decide on the size and shape of the standard and the kind of herb you want to work with. Those with small leaves and a strong stem will produce a topiary with a dense growth and a more formal look. Larger-leafed specimens and those with more flexible stems such as scented geraniums will tend to have a looser, somewhat informal appearance. Some herbs that can be trained as standards are santolina, rosemary, scented geraniums, myrtle, lavender, bay, curry plant, and lemon verbena.

Begin by finding a small plant with a strong, straight stem at the nursery or find a suitable herb from which you can take a good strong

17

upright cutting. If you are starting with a cutting, dip the end in a growing hormone and set it in perlite in a small pot until a root system has formed. Place the rooted cutting or the nursery plant in a 4-inch pot filled with a good potting mixture from the nursery or mix your own using 3 parts of loam, 1 part compost or peat moss, and 1 part builder's sand or perlite. A small standard can probably start and finish in the same pot; a larger topiary will need to be repotted as the plant grows.

Place a stake in the pot close to the stem. For a small standard, the stake should be the height of the finished tree; a bigger tree can be restaked when

it is repotted. Tie the stem to the stake loosely with a piece of wool or soft string. As the tree grows, continue to tie the stem to the stake every 4 inches. Trim all side branches from the stem for a small tree; leave the top 3 to 4 inches of foliage, trimmed to within an inch of the stem, for a larger tree. (Let any leaves growing along the stem remain to provide the plant with nourishment as it continues to grow.)

Place the topiary where it will get at least 6 hours of sun a day, turning it often so the stem stays straight. Fertilize the plant about every three weeks with a high-nitrogen fertilizer to encourage leaf growth. Continue to keep the side branches below the top growth trimmed off until the plant reaches the desired height, repotting as necessary. It is also wise to replace the light potting soil mixture with heavier soil as the plant gets larger in order to keep it from tipping over as it becomes too top-heavy.

When a small standard has reached the desired height, pinch out the growing tip to produce two branches. A small tree of a quick-growing plant such as scented geranium might only take 6 to 8 months to reach an attrac-

As fragrant as it is pretty, this lavender standard set on a birch stem, *far left,* looks especially appealing in an antique sponge-ware pitcher. The Styrofoam ball was covered with moss before the individual stems of lavender were inserted so any small gaps would not be noticeable.

Below, prostrate rosemary is trained around a spherical topiary form. A grouping of myrtle and rosemary standards in antique English pots share a table in Chris Mead's bedroom, *opposite,* with a collection of old decoys. The topiaries range in age from 2 to 7 years.

section but keep them trimmed close to the stem. When the stem has reached its finished height, pinch out the growing tip and begin the pruning process over the entire length of the foliage. The more you prune, the denser and more attractive the head will be.

If you would like to grow a standard with a double or triple ball, allow stem growth to develop along the stem where the second and/or third ball will be but continue to remove all stems between the balls. When the topiary has reached its desired height, prune each ball as above.

tive height, while a larger tree of slow-growing myrtle could be a matter of years. After these new shoots have produced several sets of leaves, you can remove the leaves from the main stem. Continue to prune the developing branches as they grow. For each inch or two of growth, trim back by half, allowing more branches to form until you have a well-formed ball—or square or cone if that is your preference.

With a larger plant, wait until the stem below the foliage reaches the height you want beneath the head. Tie a ribbon around the stem below the leaves to mark the point, then let the stem continue to grow until the height above the ribbon is the height you want the ball to be. Do not remove the side branches from this

20

A variety of shapes densely covered with rosebuds and set in a collection of antique white pitchers look equally handsome grouped together or used singly. Start with various sized Styrofoam balls or with circles, hearts, or other shapes cut from a piece of Styrofoam board. Cover them with moss, then add the rosebuds with a hot-glue gun. Set on a moss-covered dowel. *Opposite,* an old-fashioned apple bucket makes a perfect container for this colorful kitchen topiary combining bay, thyme, lavender, pomegranates, cinnamon sticks, and gingerroot. The moss-covered Styrofoam ball has been set on a bunch of long cinnamon sticks, then covered with bay sprigs interspersed with bunches of thyme or lavender wired to florist's picks. Finally, the decorative pomegranates and spices have been affixed with a hot-glue gun.

Once a topiary has reached its final size, it need not be repotted, but you must continue to trim it to keep the shape neat.

You can also train herbs into ring shapes. Take an old wire hanger or some heavy wire and bend it into a circle of the size you want with 4 to 6 inches extra at each end. Twist these two ends together and stick them into a pot next to an herb that has a rather trailing growth, such as prostrate rosemary or lemon crispum geranium. Prune off all but the two strongest stems and begin training the remaining shoots around the circle, tying them to the wire every few inches. Prune any side shoots as the plant grows around the wire until you have a nice bushy circle.

dried topiaries

When live topiaries are not practical because you haven't enough light or enough time to care for them, consider one of dried herbs and everlastings; they can be equally delightful and as fanciful as you please. Try red peppers or bay for a kitchen topiary;

23

Any cook would love this whimsical garlic topiary, *above,* set in an antique canister. Attach whole heads of garlic to a Styrofoam ball with a hot-glue gun, holding them in place until the glue dries; then fill in any spaces between the heads with whole nutmegs. A dowel covered with allspice acts as a stem; rose hips cover the base instead of the more expected moss.

Lush and feminine, this rose-studded topiary also contains larkspur, hydrangea, artemisia, carnations, and wheat, all of which have been applied to a moss-covered Styrofoam ball with a hot-glue gun. The ribbon-wrapped dowel stem is very much in keeping.

turn a bouquet of full-blown roses from the garden into a glorious decoration for a special celebration, or create a lollipop tree of dried lavender so fragrant it will scent an entire room.

Topiaries of dried materials are relatively quick and easy to make. The two basic methods of construction differ only in one aspect: the foundation for the head. Depending on whether your topiary will incorporate dried or live material, you can use either a Styrofoam ball or cone that has been covered with moss or painted green, or a chicken wire shape stuffed with Oasis. Styrofoam shapes are preferable if you plan to attach dried material with a hot-glue gun, wire it to florist's picks, or if the material has good strong stems, such as bay or rosemary. A wire-covered Oasis form is better for fresh herbs and flowers, which have weaker stems, or if you want to make an oversized or unusually shaped topiary.

A bay tree topiary to brighten up a kitchen is simple to make. Start with a moss-covered Styrofoam cone. Put a spot of white glue at one end of a fresh bay leaf and affix it to near the bottom of the cone so that the other end protrudes just a bit below the bottom of the cone. Continue around the bottom, then start another layer of leaves a little above the first. Repeat until you reach the top, finishing off with the smallest bay leaves you have. As the leaves dry they will curl slightly, giving the tree its nice texture.

Whichever method you elect to use, decide on the size and shape of the topiary and on the materials and general effect before you select your base. Remember that the finished topiary may be considerably larger than the bare frame, depending on the materials it is covered with. A moss-covered shape with just a few small rosebuds will remain close to the original size; one spiked with sprigs of bay or lavender becomes at least several inches larger all around.

If you decide to use a Styrofoam shape, either spray-paint it and allow it to dry or, using white glue, cover it carefully with sheet moss. In either case, the green background will make any small holes in the material less

Simple geometric shapes take on a formal air when decorated with precise patterns of rosebuds, *left.* These use a Styrofoam sphere and a cone glued on top of a cube. Using white glue, cover the shapes with moss. Keeping the finished pattern in mind, add the rosebuds to the moss-covered forms with a hot-glue gun. For variety, cover the forms with potpourri or dried herbs instead of moss. Fragrant potpourri pomanders from Meadowsweet Herb Farm are made by coating Styrofoam balls in white glue, then rolling them in a colorful potpourri. You may need to fill in any holes with additional glue and repeat the process. Heap them in a bowl to add their scent to the room.

apparent. This is particularly important when you are covering the entire sphere with an herb whose head is larger than the stem, such as lavender. An Oasis and chicken wire frame is made by cutting the Oasis into roughly the shape you want. (To obtain a large enough piece, you may have to tape several pieces of Oasis together.) When you have the approximate shape, cut a piece of chicken wire and bend it around the Oasis. Bind it shut with waterproof tape or by twisting the ends of the cut wire together.

Right: **To make this pretty topiary in shades of pink and yellow, large rosebuds were attached to a moss-covered Styrofoam form with a hot-glue gun. A twig stem and bits of curly vine inserted in the pot add more charm.** *Opposite,* **a yarrow topiary in a miniature Versailles planter complements a collection of majolica.**

The double heads, inspired by the forked birch log stem, were made by inserting stems of yarrow into a Styrofoam ball; any spaces were filled in with additional yarrow applied with a hot-glue gun.

Once the base for the head is ready, select a stem that will be in proportion. This can be a thin birch branch, a bunch of cinnamon sticks, a dowel wrapped in moss—anything that seems appropriate and is strong enough to support the finished head. (Again, remember that the head will be somewhat larger after the material has been affixed.) Next, choose a pot or container that is suitable in size and feeling: a beautiful porcelain pot for a rose topiary or perhaps an apple bucket for a kitchen topiary. Find an inexpensive terra-cotta pot or a plastic container that will fit neatly inside and act as a liner. This liner will then be filled with plaster of Paris, which anchors the top-heavy standard and keeps it from falling over. It's wise to use a liner because the plaster heats up and expands as it sets, and might break the outer pot if poured directly into it. Using another pot also allows you to change containers whenever you want.

Mix the plaster of Paris (available at hardware and paint stores) according to the instructions on the package and pour it into the liner. Insert the stem

Stylized bay cones and spheres make handsome decorative accessories atop a desk. Starting at the top, apply flexible fresh bay leaves in an overlapping pattern with white glue, holding each in place briefly until the glue sets. Finish the bottom of the cone with a horizontal ring of leaves and cover the base with green felt.

into the plaster and let it set. It will set within 20 minutes and be completely hardened in 6 to 8 hours. Once the stem is set, push the head on, centering it carefully. The standard is now ready to be decorated.

If you are using a combination of stemmed sprigs and unstemmed materials such as flowers, nuts, or pomegranates, begin by inserting the sprigs directly into the form individually or in bunches. Smaller sprigged material such as thyme can be wired to a florist's pick before insertion for greater stability. Once the stemmed material is in place, the remaining decorations can be affixed with a hot-glue gun. When there is no stemmed material, glue the flowers, pine cones, or other material directly to the form. Place the finished topiary in the outer container, wedging the liner in with bits of Oasis or Styrofoam. Cover the plaster with moss to give the topiary a finished look.

It is also possible to create a topiary by setting a round or cone-shaped form directly into a pot or even setting a ball, cone, or square directly on a table without benefit of a pot. This type of topiary seems to work better with a more stylized treatment such as geometrically designed rosebuds over moss or overlapping bay leaves. Finish off the bottom of the form with a piece of green felt.

Kitchen topiaries can be made from culinary herbs. To make the subtly colored, rather roughly textured tree, insert sprigs of sage and apple mint into a Styrofoam cone in overlapping layers, starting from the bottom. For the wild marjoram bush, masses of the purple blossoms are glued to a Styrofoam ball. The chile tree is a simple matter of gluing peppers to a cone form in overlapping circles. The pots are coated with silver king artemisia applied with white glue.

BOUQUETS & ARRANG

One of the loveliest ways to spend a warm summer morning is walking through the garden in search of fragrant herbs and colorful flowers with which to create a deliciously scented bouquet. It might be nothing more than a jug of basil or mint to set on a windowsill where gentle breezes will waft its fresh aroma through the house. (According to folklore, it also banishes flies.) Or you might be inspired to assemble a little nosegay to give to a friend or a generous bouquet to adorn your mantel or dining table.

It's a joy to choose among herbs whose leaves are lacy, spiky, rounded, velvety, leathery, or smooth as silk; to combine different colors, from the deep maroon of purple basil and red sage to the silvery gray of artemisia and lavender, the dark green of germander, the bright green of santolina, or the yellow leaves of golden marjoram. But this is just the beginning: flowers, herbal and otherwise, add another dimension. Whether delicate like valerian or showy like Italian bugloss, they contribute color, shape, and often more fragrance. Wildflowers picked on the roadside, grasses, and even vegetables can be used for greater variety, enabling you to create an arrangement to suit any room, any occasion.

Pick your herbs and flowers at their peak, preferably in early morning or late afternoon. If possible, take a bucket of water with you to the garden and plunge the stems into it immediately. When you return to the house, carefully remove any foliage that will be below the water line. Using a sharp knife or clipper, cut the stems at an angle to allow them to absorb as much water as possible and quickly return the herbs and flowers to a container of warm water. (The stems absorb warm water faster than cold.)

If you preserve some of your harvest for dried arrangements, you can prolong the pleasures of the garden through the winter. They are just as decorative and far longer lasting than fresh and will add color and warmth to your house on even the snowiest winter day. Like fresh arrangements, they can be dramatic and stylized or have the natural feeling of an armful of flowers just picked from the garden and they can be used in every room from bedroom to kitchen. Make a nosegay of moth-repelling herbs such as santolina and lavender to hang on a closet door, a bouquet of bay, sage, and other culinary herbs to grace your kitchen, and a striking arrangement of wheat, lavender, and roses to set in your fireplace instead of the more expected magnolia leaves.

Peonies, once used medicinally, are purely decorative when they are dried and packed neatly into a round basket, *opposite.* **An old wheelbarrow filled with potted plants,** *below,* **is a decorative accent in the garden or on a patio.**

Arrangements of dried herbs and flowers, *left* and *above*, can be a colorful addition to any room.

Rather than fill your fireplace with the usual magnolia leaves or a fireboard during hot summer days, try a stylized arrangement of moss, statice, dried roses, and wheats like this one by Flowers Forever, *opposite*. Put a layer of Oasis in the bottom of the basket; mark the pattern on the Oasis; then carefully insert the dried materials, which have been precut to graduated heights.

A collection of old watering cans make splendid containers for herbal bouquets, which can contrast yellow and pale greens of yarrow, roses, lady's mantle, and angelica with deep purples of catnip, Italian bugloss, and lamb's ears; be a sophisticated blend of white, gray, and green with roses, dianthus, valerian, white sage, and southernwood; or blend the pinks and purples of cosmos, roses, sage, pinks, and heliotrope.

Whether your bouquet is fresh or dried, start by selecting a container that is compatible with the feeling you are trying to create. Pitchers are among the most charming containers for anything from a miniature bouquet to an imposing arrangement for a large room. Imagine a simple white china pitcher with a fresh country bouquet or dried arrangement reminiscent of the fields. An elegant porcelain cachepot would lend an air of sophistication to the most casual arrangement of roses and herbal greenery. Handsome baskets are perfect for both dried and fresh arrangements of any kind (fresh bouquets will require a waterproof liner), while a small urn might lend itself better to a more formal bouquet. Go beyond the expected when choosing a container: put a glass vase inside an old apple bucket; use mugs, teacups, or old bottles for small arrangements; cover a basket in moss; arrange a country bouquet in an old watering can or a stoneware crock.

The selection of colors and ma-

terials will play an important part in determining the overall feeling of the arrangement, too. A mixture of simple herbs in bright, contrasting colors—the clear red of a poppy, the bright blue of borage, the cheery yellow of sunflowers, and the bright green of mints and other leaves, for example—will have a more informal feeling than a bouquet of roses, pinks, and peonies in subtle tones of red and pink.

In arranging the herbs and flowers, remember that the size and shape of the bouquet must balance well with that of the container: a short, wide arrangement would look ungainly in a tall narrow container, a tall bouquet awkward in a squat vase. Decide in advance if you want your bouquet to be loose or rather controlled. A collection of grasses, wildflowers, and herbs would be good choices for a wispy, casual bouquet, while yellow roses, sage, lady's mantle, yarrow, and foxglove in a closely packed arrangement with a definite triangular or rounded shape makes a more formal presentation.

Begin the arrangement by placing the longest, biggest stems in the container to create a basic outline. If the stems are strong as are those of roses, sage, or lavender, for example, they can be placed into the container so the stems cross, making a natural structure for the rest of the material. Or you can use florist's Oasis, chicken wire, or a frog. For dried arrangements, it is definitely easier to work with an Oasis base. Once the framework has been established, fill in with the remaining material, placing the bulkier pieces in first and saving the more delicate flowers and accents until last.

of yarrow, roses, hydrangea, larkspur and weeds and grasses gathered from the fields would be perfect in a country room. *Below left,* a charming heart-shaped basket lined with moss and filled with dried roses secured with hot glue makes a lovely gift. Glue overlapping rose leaves to the edge for a finishing touch. Pat Petrondi arranges her garden bouquet in an old stoneware crock, *below.* The shape is charmingly asymmetrical; the colors a simple blend of pink, purple, and white.

Karen Cauble's antique painted basket filled to the brim with chamomile, *opposite,* has an attractive country air. *Above,* this dramatic but informal bouquet

Above: An anti-moth bouquet on your closet door adds a decorative note while it does its work. Use mothfighting herbs such as santolina, tansy, lavender, southernwood, mint, or rosemary. Dozens of dried roses gathered in a moss-covered basket, *right,* are an extravagant present. Dry the roses, leaves and all, by hanging them upside down in a cool, airy spot out of direct sunlight. Cover an inexpensive basket with moss, fill it with Oasis, and insert the roses, mixing colors and heights in a pleasing manner.

DRIED GLOBE ARRANGE-MENT IN A WHEAT-COVERED CONTAINER

Wheat stalks and a profusion of colorful dried flowers transform an inexpensive Styrofoam ball set in a metal can into a charming accent bouquet. Find a Styrofoam ball that fits inside the top of a cut-off coffee can or other wide-mouth metal container so only half of the sphere protrudes above the rim. (You can cut down a larger ball if necessary.) Remove the ball and wrap one strip of double-faced tape around the center of the can. Next, working in sections, apply a strip of hot glue at the top and the bottom and carefully press on a single layer of wheat stalks with the heads extending above the top of the can. Trim the bottoms of the stalks to be even with the bottom of the can. When the wheat is in place and the glue has dried, carefully bend back the wheat heads and reinsert the Styrofoam ball. Apply the flowers to the ball with a hot-glue gun, clustering two or three similar flowers together. Glue on more wheat heads to make a generous frame for the bouquet, then tie with a piece of braided raffia. Cover the bottom of the can with green felt.

Right, **A dried bouquet of roses, pink bachelor's buttons, and carnations dried in silica gel. *Far right,* a formal arrangement of subtly colored roses and hydrangea complements the shape of the urn.**

Tussie-mussies can be as varied as the contents of the garden. This fresh tussie-mussie of furry gray lamb's ears, mint, scented geranium leaves, and various herbs surrounding a rose, *left,* is especially charming displayed in an antique blue-and-white pitcher. A tussie-mussie for a cook, *far right,* combines spicy bay, allium blossoms, and thyme with cinnamon, ginger, and other spices.

The word "tussie-mussie" is simply an old-fashioned name for little nosegays of aromatic herbs and flowers. In medieval England both men and women carried tussie-mussies made from strongly scented herbs such as rosemary and thyme; they masked unpleasant street odors and, according to doctors of the day, helped protect them from the plague. In 1718, however, Lady Montagu published her book, *The Language of Flowers,* and English nosegays suddenly took on a more romantic air. The book was inspired by a trip to Turkey where Lady Montagu had discovered the Turkish custom of assigning a meaning to herbs and flowers—a rose for love, sage for health, lemon verbena for enchantment, marjoram for blushes, for example. In that country, she reported, this fanciful language was used to "quarrel, re-

proach, or even send letters of passion, friendship or civility, or even of news without even inking your fingers." As she shared her knowledge at home, these sweet floral messages of love and friendship became the rage in both France and England, where ladies often wore them over the heart in a decorative holder also known as a tussie-mussie. By Victorian times, when it was considered unseemly to overwhelm a lady with spoken terms of endearment, these little bouquets were as common as handbags

tussie-
mussies

49

are today. They remain a lovely way to send a message of love and cheer to a sick friend, of welcome to a guest or thanks to a hostess, or of congratulations to a bride or graduate. All it takes is a quick trip to your garden to snip a rose and some stems of fragrant greenery.

Traditionally all tussie-mussies, fresh or dried, are made by surrounding a rose or other flower with concentric circles of contrasting leaves and flowers. The stems of each circle should be tightly bound with wool as you go, and the last circle should be of a fragrant large-leaved herb such as a rose-scented geranium so the fragrance will be released by the warmth of your hand.

The stems of a fresh tussie-mussie can be wrapped with damp moss or a damp paper towel and then, if you desire, bound with florist's tape. This wrapping is not necessary with dried materials or if you plan to put the nosegay in water. Finally, the stem is inserted through a hole in the center of a pretty paper doily or some lace or other pretty fabric is gathered around the stems and tied with a ribbon. If you make your fresh tussie-mussie of herbs and flowers that dry well such as fragrant rosemary, silvery artemisia, sweet-smelling roses, and pungent sage, the recipient will be able to enjoy its beauty, fragrance, and sentiment for a long time.

An old-fashioned nosegay from Meadowsweet Herb Farm includes lavender and roses wrapped in lace and tied with satin ribbon.

Opposite: **Pots of lavender, antique English flowerpots and urns, garden ornaments, and other garden-related items are artfully arranged in an old Welsh cupboard.**

A SHORT LESSON IN THE LANGUAGE OF HERBS AND FLOWERS

The many books published on this subject frequently offer differing interpretations of particular herbs and flowers. (Basil, for instance, can signify both love and hatred.) To make sure you and your friend are ''speaking'' the same language, it might be wise to include a card explaining the sentiment along with your tussie-mussie.

AGRIMONY
thankfulness

ANGELICA
inspiration, soaring thoughts

BASIL
animosity, hatred; love

BORAGE
courage; cheerfulness; brusqueness

BUGLOSS
falsehood, lies

CHAMOMILE
patience, fortitude; meekness, humility; energy in adversity

CORIANDER
hidden qualities; merit

CORNFLOWER
delicacy

DAISY
delay; wantonness

DANDELION
oracle; absurdity

DITTANY
birth

ELDER
sympathy, compassion; zeal

FENNEL
strength; worthiness; flattery, dissemblance

FEVERFEW
protection

FOXGLOVE
sincerity; insincerity, fickleness

HELIOTROPE
constancy, devotion, eternal love

HONEYSUCKLE
bonds of love; generosity; devotion

HOPS
injustice

HYSSOP
sacrifice

IRIS
message; hope; light; power; eloquence; ardor

IVY
fidelity, tenacity; friendship; marriage

JASMINE
happiness, joy; sensuality; elegance; admiration; amiability

LAVENDER
luck; silence; sad refusal; distrust

LEMON VERBENA
enchantment

MALLOW
delicate beauty; mildness

MARIGOLD
cares; sorrow; jealousy; joy; remembrance; mental anguish

MARJORAM
maidenly innocence; happiness; courtesy; blushes

MEADOWSWEET
uselessness

MINT
cheerfulness; wisdom; virtue; homeliness

MYRTLE
love; fertility; fragrance

NASTURTIUM
patriotism; affection

NETTLE
spite; slander; coolness

PANSY
memories; courtship; loving thoughts

PARSLEY
feasting; death; joy

PENNYROYAL
escape

PERIWINKLE
sweet remembrances; first love

ROSE

red, love; yellow, infidelity; white, silence

ROSEMARY

remembrance

RUE

contrition, repentance; grief; mercy; pity; purification

SAGE

love; health; esteem; domestic tranquility and virtue

SALAD BURNET

merry heart; gaiety; joy

SOUTHERNWOOD

jest, bantering

TANSY

"I declare war against you"; refusal

VALERIAN

an accommodating disposition, concealed merit

VIOLET

innocence; modesty; humility; loyalty, faith, steadfastness

WORMWOOD

absence; sorrowful parting

YARROW

war

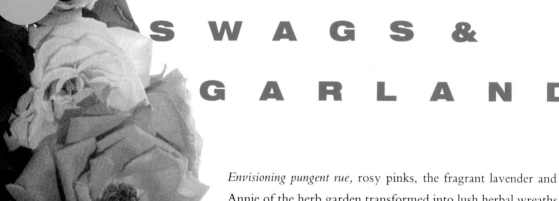

SWAGS & GARLANDS

Envisioning pungent rue, rosy pinks, the fragrant lavender and bushy sweet Annie of the herb garden transformed into lush herbal wreaths and garlands for the house adds an extra dimension of pleasure to summer gardening. When faced with a determinedly spreading mass of silver king artemisia, gathering the subtle gray sprigs for a wreath is a much more rewarding task than simply thinning the plants. An impressive cluster of yarrow growing at the back of a border stirs thoughts of wreaths in the golden tones of fall. Glorious roses in full bloom might suggest an enchanting swag to hang over a mirror or a window in the bedroom. Once you begin to see your garden as a source for herbal decorations, you will find inspiration everywhere.

Bunches of fresh sage, rosemary, and thyme are wired to a vine wreath to hang in the kitchen. For parties, it can be decorated with a few white roses.

Meadowsweet Herb Farm's culinary wreath starts with a spiky circle of cinnamon sticks glued to a twig or Styrofoam base. Dried ginger-root, rose hips, nutmegs, cardamom pods, dried chile peppers, and star anise are glued in a pleasing arrangement on top.

The curved and pointed shapes of chile peppers lend this wreath an interesting shape and texture. With a large-eyed needle and a piece of string, pierce the broad end of the peppers and gather a few of them together into a bunch. Make enough bunches to cover a wire or vine wreath form and wire them on.

wreaths

The most familiar of all herbal decorations, wreaths are also the most versatile. A bride might wear a charming circlet of delicate herbs and flowers over her veil much the way Greek heroes sported garlands of bay; a composition of more dramatic materials might be bound into a glorious wreath to hang over a fireplace or in a window. Wreaths can be as simple and spontaneous as a few sprigs of fresh lavender, rosemary, or any other leaves or flowers you fancy clipped on the spur of the moment and tucked into a little twig circle to set around a candle on the dining room table or hang on the wall of a summer cottage.

They might be made of beautiful fresh roses for a special occasion or simply masses of one herb such as sage or marjoram. When summer ends there is nothing more satisfying than creating a wreath from the contrasting textures and colors of a carefully dried harvest to complement a room or celebrate special events and holidays. Imagine, for example, a wreath of dried pink roses, soft gray lamb's ears, and perhaps a few pinks to welcome a new baby girl. Or a wreath of thyme, bay, or marjoram decorated with hot peppers, garlic, and other culinary herbs as a present for your favorite cook. Materials can range from goldenrod and other wildflowers and weeds picked from the roadside to earthy chive flowers and pungent santolina. Whether wreaths are minuscule or oversized, round or heart shaped, formal enough in feeling to fit effortlessly into an elegant sitting room or carefree enough to be right at home in the humblest cottage, there is no better way to bring the color and warmth of the herb garden indoors.

A wreath of herbs and flowers by Sonoma Flower Company is reminiscent of a lovely English chintz. German statice was used as the base, herbs and flowers were added with a hot-glue gun.

Whole heads of garlic, dried red peppers, and bits of yarrow, *left,* add color to this kitchen wreath from Fredericksburg Herb Farm. Bunches of sage, thyme, lavender, purple basil, and other culinary herbs are wired to a straw base, then the decorative touches are added with a hot-glue gun. Lush and colorful, this living wreath, *above,* is a glorious centerpiece, especially when set around a large blue-and-white porcelain jar instead of the more usual candle. Betsy Williams fashions tiny rosebuds into miniature heart wreaths, *right,* to tie around a pretty napkin, scent a hanger, or hang on a tree.

MAKING WREATHS

To make a wreath you need just a few basic materials: a straw or metal wreath form, Styrofoam shape, or simple twig wreath; moss to cover the form if desired; glue, florist's pins or fine wire to attach the materials; and a generous supply of the herbs and flowers you plan to use.

For wreaths of dried herbal materials, a straw wreath form is probably the simplest to work with and will most easily produce a full, lush finished product. Individual bunches of the dried material you select can be attached directly to the form with florist's pins or by wrapping fine florist's wire or nylon fishing line over the stems as you work your way around the wreath.

A metal form will have to be covered with sheet moss or sphagnum moss (available from a florist) bound on with nylon fishing line before you begin to attach your herbs. Styrofoam forms should also be covered with sheet moss, but it can be attached with white glue rather than fishing line. With a twig

wreath, materials can be wired directly to the base.

If you want to make a wreath of living materials such as bay or summer herbs and flowers, fill a metal form with damp spaghnum moss or a wet oasis form from the florist. Wrap it completely with green florist's tape, barely overlapping the edges so that it will not be too thick for the stems to penetrate.

Whichever type of base you choose, be sure to attach a loop of wire for hanging before you begin to affix the materials.

Once you've prepared your base, there are two basic approaches to wreath making. The most common technique involves covering the entire base with a single type of herb. Choose one that is full and dries well such as silver king artemisia, sage, or sweet Annie. Your choice will depend in part on the color and look you want to achieve. It's preferable to use fresh material for the base, as it is less fragile to work with, but it will shrink as it dries, so allow plenty of fullness to compensate.

Gather a bunch of the chosen

herb and wire or pin it to the outside edge of the wreath. Place a second bunch on the outside edge overlapping the first so the stems of the first bunch are concealed. Continue around the wreath, overlapping the bunches with all bunches facing in the same direction so the stems are hidden, and tuck the stems of the last bunch under the leaves of the first. Repeat on the inner edge, then on the top. Once the base is completed, let it dry flat to prevent the herbs from drooping. This should take from one to two weeks depending upon the material and the weather. When it is thoroughly dry, decorate with sprigs or bunches of other fresh or dried herbs, flowers, or spices. These can be added individually or wired together, then wired to a florist's pick or attached with florist's pins or a hot-glue gun.

An alternate method is to design three or four different bunches of mixed herbs and flowers using different colors and textures to create pleasing arrangements. The designs should complement one another and can be all dried or a mixture of fresh

A wreath of fresh roses is an exquisite decoration for a party and very easy to make. Cut the rose stems just long enough to reach the wire form's Oasis-filled center, then arrange the roses around the wreath, alternating colors in a pleasing way. Tuck a few rose leaves between them to fill any spaces or for effect. The same look could be achieved with full-blown roses dried in silica gel and glued to a moss-covered straw wreath form.

Wreaths needn't be restricted to doors. *Right,* a wreath ornaments the door of a grandfather clock. The base of this wreath, wider at the bottom, was cut from a sheet of Styrofoam and covered in moss. Silica gel–dried roses and air-dried rose leaves were then affixed with a hot-glue gun. This simplest of wreaths, *opposite, top left,* is fashioned from chamomile blossoms wired to a straw form. Karen Cauble has finished it off with an equally simple bow of white woven tape.

For a colorful fall display, fashion a wreath of sage, yarrow, saffron flowers, and black-eyed Susan, *opposite, far right. Opposite below,* Wild California plants and grasses combine beautifully with roses, lavender, sage, and wild marjoram for a colorful wreath by Sonoma Flower Company that retains a feeling of the fields. The basic materials were wired to a twig base in a spiral pattern; then the roses were attached with a hot-glue gun.

62

No matter which method you use, if you have included any fresh herbs, allow the wreath to lie flat for a week or two until they have dried to prevent them from drooping.

Fresh wreaths are generally made for a special occasion such as a wedding or an important dinner. Materials to be used in these wreaths must have stems that are strong enough and long enough to go through the florist's tape that covers the form and into the wet medium which will keep them fresh. Roses, lavender, and lady's mantle flowers or greenery such as mint, sage, thyme, rosemary, or marjoram are just a few of the plants you might consider using. After preparing a moss or Oasis-

and dried material. Once you are satisfied, make enough bunches to cover the wreath. The total number will depend on the size of the bunches as well as the size of the wreath. Keep the bunches short enough so that they follow the curved line of the wreath easily. Wire them to the base in an eye-pleasing arrangement, following the same design all the way around the wreath. Bunches can be assembled one day and the actual wreath making can be done later. For a simpler wreath, use a single herb in each of the three bunches and rely on contrast in textures and color—the gray of sage, the green of thyme, the red of peppers—to provide interest.

filled wreath base, formulate a clear idea of the effect you wish to achieve and then begin inserting the plant material. Apply the basic greenery first, then add flowers and other accent foliage.

The Oasis or moss must be kept damp in order to keep the wreath fresh, so it should be placed on a waterproof dish before being set on a table, or be allowed to drain before hanging it. This type of wreath offers an extra bonus: if you use cuttings from easily rooted plants such as mint or scented geraniums, by the time you are ready to dispose of the wreath, you may discover that you have some cuttings ready to pot up for your garden or friends.

swags & garlands

Swags and garlands are variations on the wreath and even more versatile. Although we are accustomed to using garlands of greenery on mantels and over pictures and windows at holiday time, we don't often think of using them the rest of the year. But a mantel garland of deep purple dried sage blossoms, burnt orange

saffron flowers, golden wheat, and other richly colored materials adds a warm decorative touch during the long, cold winter and serves as a pleasant reminder of spring as you glance through seed catalogues in front of the fire. A swag full of roses, carnations, calendulas, or other herbal flowers could make a

framed floral print or a simple mirror very special. Swags and garlands can also emphasize an architectural detail: run them along chair rails, shelves, the tops of cabinets, or just beneath the ceiling where they become a colorful mock molding. Hung over a door, garlands signal a cheerful welcome to friends; in

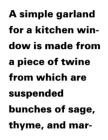

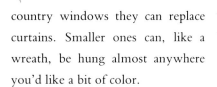

country windows they can replace curtains. Smaller ones can, like a wreath, be hung almost anywhere you'd like a bit of color.

You can make garlands flexible enough to curve around windows or pictures or rigid so they fit neatly over doors and atop mantels. To create a flexible base for a light-

weight garland, start with a piece of heavy string or a piece of wire. If you expect to use a substantial amount of material, you may need to choose something heavier, such as braided raffia or sea grass. Cut the base to size, allowing enough full-ness for graceful swags and, if you want them, a drop at either end. For

A room looks even warmer and more welcoming with a garland decorating the mantel, *left* and *above right*. The base herbs are wired to a length of braided sea grass; the rest were applied with a hot-glue gun. Herbs and flowers strung on a length of string, *right,* are flexible enough to curl around a group of candles at a party. These garlands can be made from an assortment of what is available in the garden. It would be easiest to work with fresh material and dry the completed garland rather than try to string fragile dried leaves.

a rigid garland, cut a dowel the width of the door or window. Cover the dowel in sheet moss, affixing it with white glue, and allow it to dry. A heavy garland or swag will need wire loops for hanging; place them where you want the points between the swags to fall. Lighter garlands can be hung directly on small nails hammered into the wall.

From that point forward, the procedure is the same for either type. Map out the basic scheme of color and materials before you start. You can work with a base of a single herb such as silver king artemisia, thyme, or sage, and then decorate it with other herbs and flowers. Or you can assemble bunches of different materials such as lavender, yarrow, or poppy heads and work them into the garland in a loose pattern. The width of the garland will depend on the size of the bunches and the fullness of the materials. Large-leafed herbs such as white sage will obviously have more heft than small-leafed thyme or rosemary. Since working the herbs in a straight line is easier than curving them around a wreath, it is just as easy and more practical to use dried material. Just be sure to keep the bunches on the short side in making a flexible swag so that when the swag curves, the plant material will easily follow the line.

Start at one end of the piece and wire on bunches of herbs and flowers, overlapping them so that the flowers or foliage of one cover the stems of the previous bunch. If your design includes a central motif, work in from each end to meet in the center or, alternatively, start in the center and work your way toward each end. Additional decorative materials, such as full-blown roses, can be affixed with a hot-glue gun once the basic garland is finished. The glue gun is also handy for filling in any holes in the base materials with additional sprigs.

Preceding page: **A pretty floral garland accents a chair rail. Start with a heavy piece of string, braided raffia, or anything flexible enough to drape but heavy enough to hold the materials. Bind on bunches of thyme, then, using a hot-glue gun, decorate the basic garland with yarrow, miniature roses, globe amaranth, and lavender. The garland of full-blown roses, hydrangea, and wheat topping this window,** *right,* **is made on a flexible base of braided raffia. You could also drape it over a mirror or picture. The roses were dried in silica gel then added to the garland with a hot-glue gun.**

SCE

HERBAL

There's no more pleasurable sight on a warm summer's day than masses of lavender in bloom, the stalks of purple blossoms swaying gently in the breeze while their fresh fragrance perfumes the air. And there's no more pleasurable task than walking in your garden among the sweetly scented roses, pungent rosemary, astringent southernwood, and refreshing mint to choose the most fragrant leaves and flowers for beautiful potpourris and aromatic sachets to bring the delightful fragrance of the garden into the house for friends and family to enjoy all through the year.

Since the earliest times, people have taken herbs from the garden, fields, and forest to scent their homes. In 3000 B.C. the Egyptians put flowers and spices in their tombs to enhance the afterlife and Cleopatra scented the sails of her barge. Romans perfumed their linens with lavender and stuffed their mattresses with dried rose petals. This extravagant filling was replaced in sixteenth-century England by the more modest lady's bedstraw and hops, an equally splendid choice since hops' soporific aroma helps induce sleep. In

medieval times royal households and simple peasants alike laid sachets among the linens and strewed pungent herbs such as rosemary and thyme on the floor where they released their fresh scent as guests trod upon them. By the Renaissance, gardens of sweet-smelling herbs such as roses and lavender were the source of potpourris to scent the house, while distilled floral waters served to perfume the ladies as well as their linens. In special walled gardens newly washed laundry was spread on sweet-smelling grass or lavender bushes to absorb their lovely scents as it dried. Later, Elizabethan and Victorian women created wonderfully subtle potpourris by mixing pungent spices and scented oils with their herbs and flowers. Indeed, until the beginning of the twentieth century few homes were without the lovely aroma of herbs.

When you harvest and dry your herbs, save the stems and other clippings for scented faggots for the fireplace, *left*. Tie them with raffia to make them more decorative. Toss them on the embers to release their pleasant scents.

Fortunately, we have recently rediscovered the extra pleasure to be derived from filling our homes with fragrance. There are so many ways to do this: a fragrant floral rinse water scenting the laundry or a bunch of lavender adding its fragrance to the closet; little sachets of moth-repellent herbs such as southernwood, tansy, or santolina tucked among precious woolens. Drawers can be lined with pretty scented paper; sachets can be hung in closets, on the arms of chairs, even on door knobs; and sweet pillows can be tucked behind the cushions where they will release their fragrance when leaned against.

Far left: Teatime is even more enjoyable when the tea cosy is stuffed with herbs and spices that release their pungent aroma when placed over the hot teapot. Betsy Williams's fragrant rose balls, *below,* are a handsome way to scent a room.

Left, eucalyptus potpourri. A large shell, *right,* is the perfect container for a seashore potpourri filled with shells and redolent of new mown hay and salt breezes.

p o t p o u r r i

Looking at a lovely bowl heaped with potpourri evokes memories of happy moments in the herb garden. It brings to mind a favorite old-fashioned rose, the aromatic flowers of the Provence lavender at the foot of the garden, and the spicily scented leaves of the mint or basil that once added its flavor to summer meals. Almost any plant in the garden can be gathered, dried, and blended into a colorful and fragrant potpourri.

SOME POTPOURRI HERBS AND FLOWERS

For Scent

Angelica	Heliotrope	Sweet pea
Anise hyssop	Lavender	Sweet woodruff
Basil	Lemon balm	Tansy
Bay	Lemon grass	Thyme
Bayberry	Lemon verbena	Scented geranium
Bee balm	Marjoram	Southernwood
Cardamom	Mint	Violet
Chamomile	Pineapple sage	
	Pinks	
	Rosemary	
	Rose	
	Sage	
	Santolina	

For Color Only (These are some of the most popular potpourri flowers, but any flower or petals that retain their color when dried can be used)

Bachelor's button	Larkspur
Celosia	Marigold
Delphinium	Pansy
Globe amaranth	Salvia
Heather	Statice
Hydrangea	Strawflower
Italian bugloss	Sunflower
Johnny jump-up	Yarrow
	Zinnia

For Texture

Baby's breath
Barks
Pine Cones
Pods
Seeds
Shells
Silver King
 Artemisia

A lavender-filled trug is edged with bunches of silvery artemisia and purple lavender applied with a hot-glue gun. A plastic lining keeps the dried lavender from slipping through the openings on the bottom. Lavender balls, right, add more fragrance. A fragrant pomander becomes a work of art when it is mounted on a cinnamon stick secured at both ends by a whole nutmeg strung on linen twine. Bay leaves and a wax seal are the finishing touches, opposite.

Invented by the French, potpourri quite literally meant "rotten pot" since the original mixtures were made from bruised rose leaves layered with salt and left to "rot" in a covered pot. When the lid was removed, the strong fragrance of these moist potpourris filled the room. Potpourri made its way to England after the Norman conquest and was enthusiastically adopted by the English who before long began concocting dry potpourris.

A potpourri can be as simple as lavender flowers or rose petals heaped in a basket. You can make special blends to celebrate holidays —sage, yarrow, and dried apples, perhaps, for Thanksgiving—and even turn a bride's bouquet into a potpourri to cherish over the years. You can create a fruity, spicy blend for the kitchen, a pungently fragrant mixture for the bathroom, or a lovely floral scent for the bedroom. And you needn't be content with placing your potpourri in bowls. Think about using shells or tightly woven lidded baskets, birch trays, or pretty glass jars as potpourri containers.

Making a potpourri is very simple and can be a delightful way to spend an afternoon. Traditional blends combine 4 to 5 cups of dried flowers, seeds, roots, and leaves of fragrant herbs; 4 to 5 tablespoons of crushed spices such as cloves, cinnamon, and star anise; ¼ to ½ cup of dried citrus peel; 2 tablespoons of a fixative such as orris root or gum benzoin to help hold the scent; and about 5 or 6 drops of essential oils to heighten the aroma. Petals of unscented flowers might be added for color. Less conventional potpourris are more adventuresome and offer a feast for the eye as well as the nose: beautiful shells, wood chips, pomegranates, fruits, and all manner of pods and cones add interesting texture to more expected herbs and flowers.

When you devise your own potpourri recipe, begin by choosing the basic fragrance you want and the herbs and/or flowers you will use to achieve it. Add any spices or citrus peel, a fixative, and any essential oils needed to finish off the scent. Next think about adding color and texture. If you are doing a lemony fragrance, for example, you might want to incorporate the yellow of sunflower petals, marigolds, or yarrow; a Christmas potpourri might use the red of rose hips, pomegranates, or celosia along with the green

An antique basket rimmed with bay, sage, roses, yarrow, wild marjoram, and boneset is a charming container for a mass of sweetly fragrant rose petals, *opposite.* Apply the herbs directly to the basket with a hot-glue gun, or edge the basket with masking tape and glue the materials to the tape to make a temporary decoration. Antique paisley sachets, *above,* are quite at home amidst a collection of old silver in the library of this country home.

of pine or cedar. Adding cones, shells, wood chips, or other bulky items will not only stretch the potpourri but make it more interesting looking. Avoid overwhelming the natural ingredients, however; if you add a large amount of unscented material, it may be necessary to add a bit more oil. Be sure all the ingredients are perfectly dry or the potpourri may develop mold. Mix the ingredients in a large glass or ceramic bowl, keeping careful notes of each addition so that you will be able to duplicate the potpourri. Store the finished potpourri in a covered container in a dark, cool place and let it age and mellow for 6 weeks, stirring or shaking it every few days.

The sweet scent of roses mixes with the warm tones of cinnamon in this traditional potpourri.

EUCALYPTUS POTPOURRI

A sharp, pungent scent for a man's bedroom or study.

2 cups rose petals
¼ cup cornflowers
¼ cup yarrow
¼ cup Roman chamomile flowers
¼ cup sage leaves
6 eucalyptus leaves, crushed
1 tablespoon gum benzoin
3 drops eucalyptus oil
3 drops rosemary oil

ROSE POTPOURRI

A lovely blend for living room or bedroom.

2 cups rosebuds and petals
1 cup lavender flowers
½ cup lemon verbena
½ cup thyme
½ cup rosemary
¼ cup orange peel
¼ cup cloves
2 tablespoons cinnamon chips
1 ounce tonka bean chips
3 drops rose oil
2 drops bergamot oil
1 drop clove oil
1 drop cinnamon oil

Herbs and spices from the pantry shelf can be blended into a fresh lemon-scented potpourri for the kitchen.

KITCHEN POTPOURRI

This is a refreshing citrusy potpourri made from culinary herbs and spices. Their natural aroma is nice even without oils and a fixative, but if you want it stronger and longer lasting, add them.

¼ cup rosemary

½ cup bay leaves

2 cups lemon verbena

Three 3-inch cinnamon sticks, crushed

1 cup lemon or lime balm

1 tablespoon whole cloves

2 tablespoons cardamom pods

Peel of 2 lemons, dried and
   cut in ½-inch pieces

¼ cup sunflower petals

6 drops lemon oil (optional)

2 drops bay oil (optional)

1 tablespoon orris root chips
   (optional)

SEASHORE POTPOURRI

This is a summery potpourri that invokes thoughts of newly mown grass and sea breezes. The cool coloring of gray greens and white with white shells and coarse salt would make it a wonderful potpourri for a seaside cottage.

1 cup sweet woodruff

2 cups Roman chamomile flowers

½ cup olive leaves (optional)

1 cup lemon grass

2 cups silver king artemisia

½ cup rock or pool filter salt (available at a
   pool store)

1 cup small wedding cake or other clam
   shells

2 tablespoons orris root chips

6 drops New Mown Hay oil (available at an
   herb shop)

2 drops rosemary oil

2 drops lemon grass oil

Don't stop at displaying potpourri in a bowl. Covering simple Styrofoam shapes with a colorful blend is an interesting variation which is particularly attractive in groups of contrasting shapes and sizes. To add variety to the shapes, combine a sphere or cone with a cube. Coat the forms with white glue and pat on the potpourri. You may have to repeat this process several times to completely cover the form. For a stronger scent, add a few drops of essential oil.

sweet bags

& sachets

Closely related to potpourris, sweet bags and sachets are filled with mixtures similar to potpourris but are traditionally finely ground. Unless the bag is going to be inserted in a sleep pillow or a hot pad where lumpiness would be unsuitable, however, there is no reason to use powdered ingredients or to pulverize the finished mixture. Sachets are as versatile as potpourris: fill them with antimoth herbs such as lavender, rosemary, and santolina to protect out-of-season clothing; with blends including woodsy vetiver, spicy bay, or pungent rosemary for a man's closet; or with sweet-smelling herbs such as lavender to tuck among lingerie and linens. Larger sachets filled with the fresh scents of lemony herbs, rose geraniums, or costmary will add a pleasant scent to a room when tied to a chair or bed or tucked behind the cushions. Or sew spicy basil, pungent thyme and rosemary, and cinnamon and cloves into hot pads for mugs and platters or a tea cozy for your favorite teapot. Each time they are used, the heat will release their subtle scent.

To make any of the following mixtures, combine all the ingredients in a ceramic or glass bowl and mix with a wooden spoon and store them in a covered container in a cool dark spot for three weeks. Shake the mixture every day or so while it mellows to help blend the fragrance.

SWEET BAG

Combine any herbs and spices that appeal to you for your sweet bags, choosing from those that seem most compatible to the spot where you plan to use them. You can use a favorite mixture in several rooms by varying the bag itself; make one bag of elegant damask for a formal living room, use a pretty piece of embroidery for a bedroom, or a gingham check for an informal country room.

1 cup costmary
1 cup lavender
1 cup orange mint
½ cup lemon geranium
½ cup rosemary
1 tablespoon orris root chips
3 drops bergamot oil
2 drops lavender oil
2 drops lemon oil

MOTH MIXTURE

Any of the moth-repellent herbs such as lavender, santolina, rosemary, southernwood, tansy, and mugwort can be used in a moth bag. You can add cedar chips and sweeter-smelling herbs such as mint, and cinnamon or cloves as well to make them more appealing to you but still anathema to the moths.

1 cup lavender
½ cup mint
½ cup southernwood
⅓ cup santolina
Two 3-inch cinnamon sticks, crushed
1 tablespoon whole cloves
½ cup cedar shavings, optional

Once the mixture has mellowed, divide it into thirds. Take each third and put it into a small bag made from a pretty fabric or set it in the middle of a pretty handkerchief or similar-sized piece of fabric with pinked edges. Tie the bag tightly around the neck with a nice ribbon or gather the handkerchief or fabric up around the herbs and tie in the same way. Tuck the bags in drawers and closets.

For a formal living room, make a sweet bag out of a beautiful silk damask and tie it with a picot-edged ribbon.

MASCULINE MIXTURE

This blend of herbs and spices is fresh and definitely not sweet. It would be suitable to hang in a man's wardrobe or on his bedpost.

1 cup vetiver

¼ cup sandalwood

¼ cup rose petals

½ cup rose geranium leaves

½ cup cardamom leaves

1 tablespoon ground mace

1 tonka bean, in chips

2 drops vetiver oil

1 drop rose geranium oil

SLEEP PILLOW

Sleep pillows are very similar to sachets. Instead of putting the herb mixture in a bag, however, it should go into a larger, flat pillow made of anything from muslin to thin cotton voile. Insert this aromatic envelope inside the case of your regular bed pillow or a special small sleep pillow.

½ cup hops

½ cup marjoram

¼ cup lime flowers (linden)

¼ cup bergamot leaves and flowers

¼ cup lavender

¼ cup chamomile

Mix all the ingredients together, crushing the leaves and flowers to eliminate any big pieces. Cut two pieces of fabric 6½ inches × 8½ inches. With right sides together, stitch around three and a half sides, allowing a ¼-inch seam. Turn the pillow right side out, fill with the sleep herbs, and whipstitch the opening closed.

HOT PAD MIXTURE

Because hot pads are used with food, the fragrant mixtures used to fill them are best made from herbs used in the kitchen, such as rosemary, thyme, lemon balm, lemon verbena, and rich spices. Use the same technique to make the tea cosy on page 74.

1 cup rosemary
½ cup thyme
½ cup lemon balm
1 tablespoon small cinnamon chips
1 teaspoon ground cloves

Cut two pieces of fabric—anything from a dish towel check to fine white linen—the size of the hot pad, allowing for ¼-inch seams on all sides. Place the two pieces of fabric right sides together and seam three sides. Turn the mat right side out. In the same fashion, make a flat muslin pillow a bit smaller than the hot pad. Stuff the muslin pillow with the herb and spice mixture and sew up the opening. Cut two pieces of cotton batting to fit inside the hot pad shell, tuck the pillow between them, and insert this "sandwich" into the open end of the hot pad. Whipstitch the open end by hand and the mat is ready for use. When you want to wash the mat or refresh the scent, simply open the end and remove the muslin pillow and batting.

LAVENDER WANDS

When the lavender is in bloom, it is enormously tempting to leave it swaying in the summer breezes where bees can nuzzle the blossoms in search of nectar and anyone passing through the garden can revel in its heady fragrance. But when you think of the pleasures dried lavender can bring during the cold months ahead, it spurs you to gather enough to dry for potpourris and aromatic lavender wands to scent rooms and closets. These wands take a bit of patience, but they are worth the effort.

19 fresh lavender stalks, cut as long as possible
4 feet of ¼-inch ribbon in the color of your choice

Strip the leaves from the lavender stalks. Leaving one end of the ribbon about 10 inches long, tie the stalks together just below the heads. Holding the flower heads in your fist, bend the stems down from the point where they are tied back over the flower heads. Secure them temporarily with a rubber band. The stalks should be evenly spaced and form a little cage for the flowers. Taking the long end of ribbon, start at the top of the cage and weave it in and out through the stalks until the flowers are completely enclosed. Remove the rubber band, wrap the ribbon around the stems several times and then, using both ends of the ribbon, tie a knot and a bow. Trim the ends of the ribbon and the stalks to even lengths.

If you don't have the patience to weave the ribbon through the stalks, use a shorter piece of ribbon and more lavender so the space between stalks is not as great. Proceed as above but once you have bent the stalks back, simply wrap the ribbon around the stems several times and tie a knot and bow. Trim.

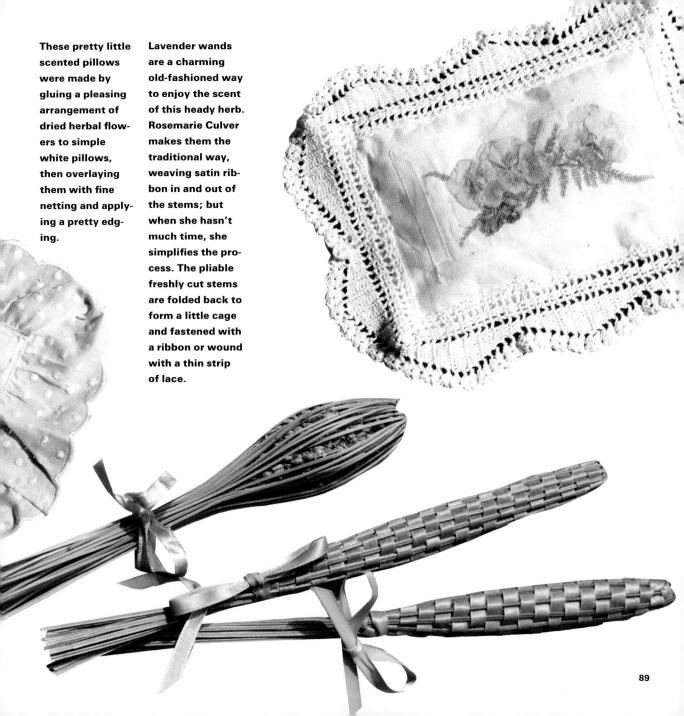

These pretty little scented pillows were made by gluing a pleasing arrangement of dried herbal flowers to simple white pillows, then overlaying them with fine netting and applying a pretty edging.

Lavender wands are a charming old-fashioned way to enjoy the scent of this heady herb. Rosemarie Culver makes them the traditional way, weaving satin ribbon in and out of the stems; but when she hasn't much time, she simplifies the process. The pliable freshly cut stems are folded back to form a little cage and fastened with a ribbon or wound with a thin strip of lace.

HERBAL

B E A U T Y

In early summer when fields and garden are abloom with elderflower, we rush to pick the delicate blossoms. Some are turned into the sweet, crispy fritters we can enjoy only a few short days each year, while others are set aside to add their softening qualities to soothing skin creams and lotions. Elderflower, however, is only one of the many herbs women have relied upon since ancient Egyptian times in their quest for soft skin, shiny hair, and alluring perfumes. Those early Egyptian beauties conditioned their hair with henna, perfumed their bodies with such herbs as myrrh and juniper, and let fragrant herbal oils soften their skin and scent their baths. In Greece courtesans used such herbs as alkanet to color lips and cheeks. Mint, fragrant roses, sweetly scented chamomile, even marjoram and lovage yielded their cosmetic benefits to the bathwater of some of the great beauties of history. The famous French courtesan Ninon de Lenclos's secret bath of mint, lavender, thyme, and rosemary with houseleeks or comfrey (depending upon the source) was rumored to be the reason she remained unwrinkled and

It's as simple to make herbal oils and vinegars, *below and opposite,* for the dressing table as it is for the kitchen.

Fragrant herbs such as lavender and roses are favored for vinegar to offset its natural pungency.

young of face to a very old age. Men, too, have luxuriated in herbal baths ever since they anointed their bodies with scented bath oils and threw lavender into the water of Roman bathhouses.

It's relatively easy to make and enjoy natural beauty products that pamper your skin and hair while enveloping you with their light herbal fragrance. Relaxing bath mixtures, soothing skin lotions, and healthful hair rinses can be made in a matter of minutes from the leaves and flowers of herbs. Packaged in beautiful old etched bottles, silver-topped jars, and pretty soap dishes, they also make lovely presents.

Since many of the most useful beauty herbs are the same ones used by cooks or in herbal decorations, you are probably already growing them. The fresh scent of mint, for example, is just as refreshing in the bathtub as in a summer drink. Each herb has its own special properties. Here is a list of some of the most popular along with their particular benefits so you can tailor your beauty potions to your special needs.

beauty herbs

CALENDULA
mildly astringent; soothes, softens, and heals the skin; highlights blond or brown hair in shampoos and rinses

CATNIP
relaxes

CHAMOMILE
lightly astringent; soothes, softens, cleanses skin; softens and adds highlights to blond and brown hair

COMFREY
heals and soothes; good for sores, burns, swellings

ELDER
softens, heals, and cleanses; has light bleaching properties

FENNEL
invigorates; lightly astringent; cleanses

HOPS
induces sleep

JUNIPER
relieves sore muscles

LADY'S MANTLE
heals; slightly astringent; good for dry skins

LAVENDER
stimulates; adds fragrance; good for oily skin

LEMON BALM
soothing and astringent; cleanses gently; fragrant

LEMON VERBENA
stimulates; fragrant

LIME FLOWERS (LINDEN)
relaxes; aids circulation

INFUSIONS AND DECOCTIONS

Herbs are most often added to beauty potions in the form of a tea. If you are using leaves and flowers, prepare an infusion by pouring 4 cups of boiling water over ¼ cup dried or ½ cup chopped fresh herbs and steep them for 20 minutes. Since it is more difficult to extract the oils from seeds, barks, or roots such as valerian, make a decoction by boiling the same quantities of materials in 4 cups of water for 20 minutes. Strain before using.

HERBAL OILS

Floral and herbal oils are delightful for their scent but those that have been infused with herbs such as rosemary or calendula also have more practical uses. Their properties and uses will vary according to the herbs used: rosemary, thyme, or lavender for massaging sore muscles, for example, or comfrey and calendula to soothe minor cuts and bruises or insect bites.

One of the simplest ways to make scented oil is to put a handful of fresh herbs or flowers in a clear glass jar early in the morning, cover them with

LOVAGE
deodorizes

MARJORAM
relieves fatigue

NETTLE
cleanses; stimulates circulation; conditions hair; fights dandruff; good for oily skin

PARSLEY
good for oily skin; adds shine to dark hair in a rinse

PEPPERMINT
refreshes and cools; heals; stimulates; astringent

ROSE
a hydrating agent that helps keep skin young looking; fragrant, slightly astringent

ROSEMARY
stimulates, invigorates; good for oily skin; gives dark hair body and shine

SAGE
stimulates; very astringent, good for oily skin; relieves aching muscles; conditions dark hair

SCENTED GERANIUMS
add fragrance

THYME
stimulates; deodorizes; antiseptic

VALERIAN
soothes nerves, soporific

YARROW
quite astringent; good for oily skin; cleanses

almond oil, and set them in the sun for the remainder of the day. The following morning strain the oil and return it to the jar with another handful of scented material. Set it in the sun again for another 8 to 10 hours. Repeat this process a total of eight times.

the bath

Turning your bath into a healthful and luxurious spa is a simple and pleasurable way to enjoy the beauty benefits of herbs. Added to your tub, they can soothe and heal weather-damaged skin, relax frayed nerves, or refresh and invigorate you when you are tired. Some help ease aching muscles and soothe sore joints while others impart a delicate fragrance to the skin.

Elderflower, left, softens and soothes in simple skin toners, cleansers, and creams; mixed with roses, lavender, and milk in bath herbs it turns an ordinary bath into a beauty treatment. Make rose and other floral waters, *far right,* by simmering 1 cup of petals in 1⅓ cups of water for 3 minutes; strain and repeat twice more, using new petals each time.

BATH HERBS

Perhaps the easiest way to add an herbal essence to your bath is with a strong infusion or decoction of bath herbs that is poured directly into the bath water. Bath bags are another way to introduce herbs into the bath. Fill little muslin bags with a handful of herbal bath mixture and tie them tightly with string. Leave one end long enough to tie the bag to the tap so the water can run through it as you fill the tub, and let the bag steep in the water while you relax and your body soaks up the herbal benefits. To get the most from the bath herbs, rub the bag all over your body before finishing your bath. Because oatmeal acts as a water softener and also soothes the skin, you might want to blend an equal amount of oatmeal with the herbs before putting them in the bag. Milk, another natural beauty aid, soothes the skin and leaves it with a lustrous finish. To add its benefits to an herbal bath, steep bath herbs in cold milk for several hours, strain, and add the herb-rich milk directly to the bath. Or mix powdered milk with bath herbs before putting them in the bath bags. And since vinegar restores the skin's natural acid mantle, adding one cupful to the bath especially during the winter months

alleviates dry, itchy, and flaky skin. Using a vinegar infused with soothing, healing skin herbs increases its beauty benefits.

Although a combination of herbs will afford more benefits, a bath based on a single herb such as rosemary or lavender can be just as pleasing. See the list on pages 92 and 93 for the general characteristics of the most popular cosmetic herbs and devise your own special mixture or get started by using one of the following recipes. Amounts are based on dried ingredients; when using plants fresh from the garden, triple or quadruple the amounts and use a bigger bag. Always blend bath herbs in a ceramic bowl and store them away from the heat in a tightly covered glass container.

BEDTIME BATH

A mixture that will help you relax and make falling asleep after a hectic day easier.

1 cup chamomile to soothe and cleanse
1 cup calendula petals to soothe and heal the skin
1 cup lime flowers for relaxation
½ cup hops to soothe the nerves and induce sleep
½ cup catnip for relaxation
1 cup lemon balm leaves for fragrance
½ cup lemon peel for fragrance

To use, place ½ cup of bath mixture in a 3-inch-square muslin bag. Tie the open end with a long piece of string.

BEAUTY BATH

This blend will leave you feeling relaxed and refreshed and your skin gently scented.

1 cup chamomile to soothe and cleanse
½ cup rose petals for fragrance
1 cup lavender to stimulate
½ cup peppermint to refresh and cool
1 cup lemon verbena for fragrance and to stimulate

To use, place ½ cup of bath mixture in a 3-inch-square muslin bag. Tie the open end with a long piece of string.

A simple herbal infusion can be used as a toner. Try sage, yarrow, or lavender for oily skin; calendula or lady's mantle for dry skin.

HERBAL SOAP

Making soap from scratch is an ambitious project that requires special ingredients such as lye and equipment that should be set aside for soapmaking only. However, you can easily make your own herbal soaps by starting with pure glycerine or castile soap and an herbal infusion. The addition of a little lanolin (available at your pharmacy) makes the soap very creamy and less drying to the skin. If you want to give the soap even more of an herbal kick, you can also stir some of the chopped herb into the soap just before pouring it into the molds.

. . . .

ROSE SOAP

You can increase the amounts of rose oil and coloring for a more intense rose impact if desired. In place of rose water you may want to try a combination of peppermint and rosemary; lemon balm or lemon verbena; orange mint; rose geranium; or lavender.

Two 10-ounce bars of glycerine soap
½–1 cup rose water (available at your
   pharmacy if you haven't enough fragrant
   roses to make it yourself [see page 94])
1 tablespoon anhydrous lanolin
10 drops rose oil
10 drops red food coloring

  Grate the soap with the grating disc of a food processor or by hand. Combine the grated soap and ½ cup of the rose water in a glass or enamel container and melt over low heat, stirring occasionally. This may take some time; adding more rose water will speed the process, but the more liquid you add, the softer the finished soap will be. When the soap is melted, stir in the lanolin, mixing well. Add the rose oil and the food coloring, stirring until blended. The herbal infusion may turn the soap the color of old oatmeal, but the addition of food coloring will remedy this. Add the coloring drop by drop so that you can control the color. Remove from the heat.

  Lightly oil several clean small round metal cans or a cut-off milk carton with almond or vegetable oil. The cans make individual soaps, the milk carton a bar that can then be cut into the sizes you want. Pour the soap into the molds, making sure there are no air bubbles. Let the soap set for a day or two before removing from the molds. At this point you can carefully cut off any marks left by the mold and cut large bars into individual cakes. Allow the soap to sit out to dry until it is quite hard.

Herbal soaps such as these of rose or a blend of rosemary and mint are easily made by melting grated castile or glycerine soap with an herbal infusion. Melt down any scraps or leftover bits with lots of water to make a gentle liquid soap to keep by the sink.

Whether you want to cleanse or moisturize your skin, forestall wrinkles, or invigorate your complexion, there is an herbal potion to fit the bill. Some herbs, such as chamomile and fennel, are cleansing; calendula, comfrey, and

skin care

elderflower are softening and soothing; and yarrow and sage have astringent qualities that are beneficial to oily skin. By combining herbal infusions with ingredients such as lanolin (available at pharmacies) and beeswax, or even chopped herbs, you can create a spectrum of herbal balms, lotions, and facial masks. In all recipes, you can tailor the herbs to your own special needs. Check the list on pages 92 and 93 for astringent herbs if you have oily skin; for those with soothing qualities if your skin is dry and sensitive. Because these creams and lotions contain no preservatives, they tend to spoil rather quickly, so it is best to make small amounts at a time and to keep them in the refrigerator when possible. Recipes that include tincture of benzoin or alcohol have a longer shelf life.

TONERS AND CLEANSERS

A strong herbal infusion can be used as a simple toner or freshener for any skin. Made with elderflower or lady's mantle, it will tend to bleach freckles; a calendula toner works on large pores and helps clear up blemishes. Keep it in the refrigerator to prolong its life and to make it even more refreshing.

Because vinegar restores the skin's protective acid mantle, it is also a good general skin toner. Gentle cider vinegars scented with lavender or roses were once part of every woman's toilette. They were patted on the brow to relieve headaches or to keep the delicate ladies of Victorian times from feeling faint. To use vinegar as a toner, dilute it by at least half or as much as 6 to 1 with spring water before using. Keep a small bottle of this diluted version on your dressing table. Never apply undiluted vinegar directly to

You can make a gentle cleanser by mixing lanolin and almond oil with an herbal infusion. If your skin tends to be oily, try using sage; elder would be a better choice for dry skin.

the skin. The more fragrant herbs such as lavender, rose, rosemary, orange mint, lemon balm, or lemon verbena are the most popular herbs to use with vinegar since their delightful fragrance overcomes the sharp smell of the vinegar. Allow herbal vinegars to infuse in the sun for at least two weeks before using the vinegar.

MOISTURIZERS

Designed to help skin retain moisture, these softeners work most effectively when applied over damp skin. Light moisturizers are generally fine in the summer when humidity is high, but during the drying days of winter a heavier, creamier moisturizer would be more effective. As with other preparations, the herb used can be varied according to your skin type.

HERBAL CLEANSER

This cleanser for dry, sensitive skins is somewhere between a cream and a lotion. If you would prefer a more liquid version, add 2 more tablespoons of almond oil and 2 of the herbal infusion. If your skin is oily, substitute an infusion of sage or yarrow. For normal skins, try rose water, or an infusion of lady's mantle or chamomile.

2 tablespoons anhydrous lanolin
¼ cup almond oil
¼ cup elderflower infusion

   Place the lanolin and almond oil in a glass or enamel saucepan over boiling water and allow it to melt. Remove from the heat and slowly beat in the infusion with an electric beater until the mixture is almost cool and very well blended. Transfer to a sterilized jar or bottle.

SCENTED VINEGAR SKIN TONER

¼ cup fresh or dried lavender
¼ cup fresh mint leaves
1½ cups cider vinegar

   Place the herbs in a jar with a cover and set in the sun for 2 to 3 weeks, turning and shaking frequently. Or bring the vinegar to a boil, pour over the herbs and let them steep, covered, until cool or overnight. Strain and pour the vinegar into a sterilized bottle. Dilute with 6 parts spring water before using.

SIMPLE SUMMER MOISTURIZER

3 tablespoons glycerine (available at your pharmacy)

2 tablespoons rose water

2 tablespoons elderflower infusion

1 tablespoon honey

Place all ingredients in a bottle and shake until well blended.

ANTIWRINKLE LOTION

Fennel is the best known wrinkle-fighting herb, but since these unwanted facial lines are often the result of dryness, roses and honey, both hydrating agents, can also be used to keep skin soft, supple, and line free. This lotion could be made with a strong infusion of chamomile or calendula or a mixture of half rose and half fennel. Make it in relatively small amounts and use sparingly around the eyes and mouth.

2 tablespoons glycerine

2 tablespoons rose water

2 tablespoons witch hazel

4 tablespoons honey

Put all the ingredients in a small bottle, cork tightly, and shake vigorously until well blended.

HAND LOTION

Your grandmother probably kept her hands soft and smooth with rose water and glycerine lotion. A similar mixture of elderflower water and glycerine is also soothing and acts as a mild bleach as well. This richer version incorporates a little oil.

Generous pinch borax (available at your supermarket)

¼ cup rose water or elderflower or calendula infusion

¼ cup glycerine

2 tablespoons witch hazel

1 tablespoon almond oil

Melt the borax in the infusion over low heat. Put the remaining ingredients in a bottle, add the infusion, and shake until well blended.

COLD CREAM

This is a general all-round cream that can be used to remove make-up or as a night cream. It contains elderflower, a gentle herb that helps soothe the skin and keep it white, but it could be made equally well with chamomile, lady's mantle, rose water, or calendula, which works especially well to quell a sunburn. If you don't want to bother with making your own cream, stir 1 tablespoon of infusion into 4 ounces of any good unscented commercial cream.

1 cup almond oil

1 ounce white beeswax

1 cup elderflower infusion

½ teaspoon borax

Place the oil and beeswax in a glass or enamel container and let the wax melt slowly over boiling water. Meanwhile, heat the infusion with the borax, stirring until the borax has dissolved. When the wax has melted, slowly pour the infusion into the wax and oil mixture, stirring constantly. Remove the cold cream from the heat and continue to beat until the cream is cool and the ingredients are completely blended.

Herbal antiwrinkle lotion and cleanser,*opposite,* and a simple summer moisturizer, *left.*

FACIAL STEAMS

Facial steams, *opposite*, made by pouring boiling water over a handful of herbs, deep-clean the face and keep skin fine textured. This mixture of calendula, chamomile, comfrey, and lady's mantle is especially good for dry skin. *Below*, a rich cold cream.

You can help keep your skin clean, soft, and smooth by the regular use of herbal steams. They will really deep-clean the skin and help refine large pores if you use them weekly. As with other herbal treatments, your skin type will determine what kind of herbs you should use: the recipe below offers formulations for both dry and oily skin. Avoid this treatment entirely if your skin is hypersensitive.

Place ¼ cup of the herb mixture in a large bowl and pour 1 quart of boiling water over it. Set the bowl on a table or counter where you can comfortably sit with your face 8 to 10 inches over the bowl. Tent your head with a large towel so the steam can't escape. Don't put your face too close to the steam. Remain as long as you are comfortable, up to 10 minutes, letting the herbal steam penetrate your pores. Rinse your face with cool water, pat dry, and moisturize.

- -

FACIAL STEAM
Choose the ingredients that best suit your skin type, either dry or oily; otherwise the method is the same.

¼ cup chamomile
¼ cup comfrey (for dry skin) or lavender (for oily skin)
¼ cup calendula (for dry skin) or lemon balm (for oily skin)
¼ cup mint (for dry skin) or nettle (for oily skin)
¼ cup lady's mantle (for dry skin) or yarrow (for oily skin)

FACIAL MASKS

Masks soothe or stimulate the skin while they clean and nourish it. You will feel especially refreshed if you take the time to lie down and rest while the mask is doing its work. As with other beauty preparations, masks can be formulated especially for your skin type according to the herbs you use.

. . . .

SIMPLE HERBAL MASK FOR ALL SKINS

For oily skins substitute finely chopped sage and sage infusion for the chamomile; for dry skin use 1 tablespoon powdered dried elderflower and one tablespoon rose water instead of chamomile.

1 tablespoon powdered dried chamomile
3 tablespoons buttermilk or yogurt
1 tablespoon chamomile infusion
2 tablespoons honey

Mix the chamomile powder, buttermilk, and honey together in a small bowl. Clean your face thoroughly and spread the mask carefully over your face, avoiding the eyes and mouth. Lie down for 20 to 30 minutes with cotton pads soaked in a chamomile infusion over your eyes. Wash the mask off with warm water, pat your face dry, and apply a thin layer of moisturizer.

Women have been using herbs to add color and shine to their hair for at least five thousand years. Although it is impossible to change hair color with an herbal rinse, you can highlight blond hair with chamomile or calendula,

h a i r   c a r e

darken hair with sage, or add a reddish tone to black hair with henna. For more shine, try parsley and rosemary, but since they tend to darken the hair, blonds might prefer to use nettles, which condition and fight dandruff. In the recipes that follow, you can substitute whichever herb works best for you, or use a combination of two. And if you really want to be completely herbal, find some soapwort root. This herb, which grows plentifully along the roadside as well as in gardens, is an effective cleanser (although it will not lather up like commercial shampoos) and is so gentle it is used in the restoration of precious old textiles.

Start with a pure castile shampoo or if you cannot find shampoo, grate some castile soap and melt it down in enough water to make it the consistency of shampoo. Then thin it further with an equal amount of herbal infusion. This shampoo will keep for only about a month so do not make more than you will use in that time.

HERBAL RINSES

An herbal hair rinse can be nothing more than a simple herbal infusion. To make it work harder, add ½ cup vinegar, effective against dandruff, for every 2 cups of infusion. Try a combination of chamomile and calendula for blond hair, rosemary and parsley for dark hair, linden if you shampoo frequently, nettles alone or combined with other herbs to fight dandruff and act as a general conditioner.

p e r s o n a l

f r a g r a n c e

It is a simple matter to make delicately scented eau de cologne, floral waters, and oils. The waters can be used for scent only or added to other herbal preparations in place of an infusion or for added fragrance. Oils can be added to the bath or used to scent the skin.

. . . .

The amounts in the following recipes are for fresh herbs. If you are using dried herbs, use only half as much.

SPICY EAU DE TOILETTE

6 tablespoons chopped angelica leaves

6 tablespoons chopped basil

2 bay leaves

2 tablespoons coriander seeds

1 nutmeg, broken into small pieces

1 tablespoon cloves

Three 3-inch cinnamon sticks, crushed

2 cups unscented rubbing alcohol or vodka

Place all ingredients in a glass jar with a tight-fitting cover. Let the jar sit in a warm place for several weeks, then strain and pour the eau de cologne into a sterilized bottle.

EAU DE COLOGNE

½ cup lavender
¼ cup rosemary
Peel of 1 lemon
Peel of 1 orange
½ cup orange mint
½ cup lemon balm
2 cups rose water
2 cups vodka

Place all ingredients in a large glass jar with a cover and let them steep for 8 to 10 days. Strain and pour into a sterilized bottle.

Make a fresh smelling eau de cologne, *left,* by soaking fragrant herbs, spices, and fresh-scented citrus in alcohol or vodka. Steeping angelica, basil, and spices in alcohol or vodka, *far left,* produces a spicy cologne suitable for either sex, *opposite.* Over-*leaf,* colognes can be sweetly floral, pungently herbal, or headily spicy.

HERBS FOR THE

HOLID

The fresh fragrance of pine and the warm spicy aroma of pomanders heaped in a bowl always stir memories of Christmas. These distinctive scents are as much a part of the holiday as the wreaths and garlands of juniper and pine, the fir trees resplendent with glittery ornaments, and the other decorations conceived with love and imagination that the celebration of Christmas always seems to inspire. Often the most charming expressions of the season are based on herbs. With their varied colors and textures and fragrant aromas, herbs can make any holiday more festive and decorative—sage, yarrow, and bittersweet at Thanksgiving, for example, or bright red field poppies and cornflowers on the Fourth of July. Yet somehow they seem to lend themselves most happily to Christmas. For the uninitiated, this might seem an unlikely time to look to the herb garden for inspiration, but herbs have been an

integral part of a traditional yuletide celebration ever since the three wise men brought frankincense and myrrh to the manger where, according to legend, Jesus lay on a pallet of lady's bedstraw.

One of the most obvious herbal choices for Christmas is rosemary, the symbol of friendship, whose fine needles and piney smell make it a delightful substitute for more traditional holiday greenery. Imagine pungent branches of rosemary bound into a garland studded with white roses, tied with gossamer gold bows, and hung over the mantel. Envision glossy bay leaves and apple slices garlanding a country window or a lush kitchen wreath of fresh bay decorated with bunches of red chiles and the dainty white flowers of garlic chives. You can make herbal garlands to festoon windows and doors; drape chandeliers, mirrors, and pictures; and decorate the mantel. Christmas wreaths welcome herbs, too. Add juniper, bay, myrtle, winterberry, and other herbs to the wreath on the front door; or fashion more delicate materials such as red roses and carnations into handsome wreaths to hang above a mantel or encircle a candle on the dining table. In fact, many of the wreaths, swags, and other herbal decorations in this book can be given a cheery holiday feeling simply by adding seasonal herbs and greenery, spices, pine cones, and rose hips.

Even the chandelier is treated to a garland in Carol Pflumm's dining room. This one is made from bay leaves, cinnamon sticks, and rose hips. At the windows holiday garlands of bay leaves and dried apple slices strung on nylon fishing line hang beneath swags of artemisia tied with red bows. A basket filled with rose hips acts as a centerpiece. The unpretentious decorations are totally in keeping with the simplicity of the room.

115

A tiny herbal wreath rings the neck of the wine decanter, *left;* sprigs of gilded rosemary are set at each place to welcome guests. Rosemary, white roses, and gossamer gold ribbon combine for glamorous Christmas effects, *right*. Fashion aromatic branches into garlands for over mirror and mantel; bedeck rosemary topiaries with gold bead swags or gold bows.

c h r i s t m a s

Filling the house with the enticing scents of Christmas—pungent bayberry, pine, and juniper, spicy cinnamon and cloves, the zesty fragrance of oranges and apples—will evoke memories of Christmases past and establish happy

f r a g r a n c e

traditions for the celebrations yet to come. Concoct a pretty and fragrant holiday potpourri of rosemary, juniper or bayberry, bay leaves, rose hips, pine cones, bits of gilt, slices of dried orange or apple, and lots of cinnamon and set it in baskets and bowls all through the house. Place a big basket of pine cones anointed with your own special blend of Christmas oil made from cinnamon, rosemary, and bergamot by the fire to toss into the embers and scent the room. Or set a bit of simmering potpourri on the back of the stove so its warm aroma can reach out to delight your family and welcome holiday visitors.

CHRISTMAS SIMMERING POTPOURRI

Let this simmer on the back of the stove to fill your house with the inviting scents of the holidays.

1 cup bay leaves, crumbled
4 fresh or dried rosemary sprigs
Six 3-inch cinnamon sticks
6 cloves
Rind of 1 orange

   Place all ingredients in a saucepan with 4 cups of water and bring to a boil. Turn the heat down and allow the potpourri to simmer on the back of the stove. Check frequently to make sure the water has not evaporated, adding more as needed.

CHRISTMAS POTPOURRI

Gild some of the bay leaves and pine cones with gold paint for extra holiday sparkle.

1 cup fresh or dried cedar tips
1 cup fresh or dried bay leaves
3 small dried pomegranates
1 or 2 dried orange slices
¾ cup dried orange peel
¼ to ½ cup crushed cinnamon pieces
2 dozen assorted pine cones of all sizes
¼ cup dried rose hips
2 tablespoons orris root chips
4 drops oil of cinnamon
2 drops bergamot oil
1 drop rosemary oil

   Combine all ingredients in a ceramic bowl. When well blended, store in a covered container in a cool, dark place for 2 to 3 weeks to mellow, shaking occasionally.

For the holidays, a collection of Santas stands on Audrey Julian's kitchen counter. Underneath, a handsome garland of boxwood, yarrow, pomegranates, dried apple slices, spice cookies, and rose hips adds a festive note.

Herbs can make that most traditional of all holiday decorations, the Christmas tree, more festive, too. Mini tussie-mussies of dried herbs and flowers transform a stately pine into a romantic fantasy; ornaments of scented beeswax or spicily scented calico candy canes and reindeer are charmingly old-fashioned. On a smaller scale, you can make everlasting trees of silver king or sweet Annie decorated with yarrow, red peppers, cinnamon sticks, and other herbs and spices, or fashion small trees of fresh rosemary and mass them together for a centerpiece. Even live topiaries take on a holiday spirit draped with gold bead garlands or beautiful ribbons.

christmas
decorations

The handsome overdoor decoration in Audrey Julian's front hall, *far left,* has its roots in Colonial tradition. It was made by cutting a piece of plywood to size, affixing a border of magnolia leaves with a hot-glue gun, then completing the design with a combination of lamb's ears, boxwood, pomegranates, cockscomb, cinnamon sticks, globe amaranth, pepper berries, yarrow, artichokes, and almonds. *Left,* Linda Kaat's imposing tree is decorated with miniature dried tussie-mussies, wreaths, and baskets of flowers. An everlasting tree, *below,* becomes a colorful Christmas decoration when Betty Baker covers it with a selection of bright herbs and flowers.

Audrey Julian makes use of the cheerful red of rose hips in decorating her old-fashioned tree, *left*. They are tucked among branches tipped with real candles and hung with dried apple slices, strings of raisins, nuts, kumquats, and cinnamon hearts. The mixed grays and greens of dried herbs and bright red cockscomb, *above*, combine in her simple country garland.

ROSEMARY CHRISTMAS TREE

These "live" trees are fresh and fragrant. Handsome centerpieces, they are equally charming in the kitchen, the bath, or anywhere you need a touch of Christmas. To make them you will need Oasis, a terracotta pot, and a good supply of fresh rosemary.

Decide what size tree you want and select an appropriate sized pot. In general, the diameter of the pot should be about half the height of the finished tree, but you can adjust this if you want an especially tall, thin tree. Cut a block of Oasis so that it is approximately cone shaped and will sit about a half inch or so down inside the rim of the pot. The rosemary will bring it out to the edge. If you are making a large tree, you may have to put several pieces of Oasis together to get the right shape. (The simplest way to do this is with toothpicks.) Once the Oasis is cut to shape and inserted in the pot, start at the base and push small, straight stems of rosemary upright into the Oasis all around the edge of the pot. The sprigs should be relatively short, no more than 2 to 3 inches long for

a small tree and proportionately longer for a bigger tree. When you have finished the first row, start a second circle inside and slightly above the first. Continue in this manner until you have reached the top. Prune any uneven edges from the tree, then wet the Oasis and keep it damp to keep the rosemary fresh. These trees can be decorated with strings of cranberries, gold beads, tiny pine cones, or rose hips.

VINE TREE

Depending on the decorations, a vine tree can be sophisticated or very country in feeling. To make one yourself, collect a mass of wild grapevines late in the summer while they are still flexible. Shape chicken wire into a cone slightly smaller than the size you want the finished tree to be. Take one of the thicker vines and attach it at the base of the cone by weaving it in and out of the chicken wire for a few inches. Continue to coil the vine around the cone, keeping the circles of vine as close together as possible. Continue up the tree, overlapping and weaving in new pieces of thick vine as needed. Leave a 6-inch piece at the top and weave that back into the top of the tree. Using slightly thinner vines, repeat the process. The second layer should thoroughly cover the cage; if it does not, you may need to repeat the process a third time. When the tree is finished, string tiny lights around it. Decorate with bunches of herbs tied with red ribbon, fresh or dried red roses (if you use fresh roses, they will probably dry in place, changing color slightly but remaining most attractive), and tiny pomanders made

from kumquats or lady apples. Top it off with a large red bow, allowing the streamers to hang down the tree. For a more country feeling, use pomegranates, scented calico ornaments, tussie-mussies of herbs, and rose hips tied with red-and-white checked ribbon.

Votive candles are encircled with bay leaves and tied with ribbon; the heat of the flame releases the bay's spicy fragrance. Audrey Julian fashions a variation on the traditional fruit tree, *above,* with dried pomegranates, yarrow, pepper berries, and box.

For a festive Christmas dinner in the country, lay the table with a beautiful old paisley shawl, then set out a stand of fragrant rosemary trees in antique terra-cotta pots. Garland paintings with rosemary and bay and place a beribboned sprig of rosemary at each place as a sign of friendship.

SCENTED BEESWAX ORNAMENTS

These charming ornaments look especially good on an old-fashioned country tree. Use them, too, as package decorations for special friends.

1 pound beeswax
2 tablespoons scented oil of your choice
Wicking or string
Tin candy molds in Christmas shapes

Place the beeswax in an old coffee can and set it in a pan of water or on top of a thick warming plate over a low flame. Allow the wax to melt slowly. While it is melting, oil the molds lightly with vegetable oil and set aside in a warm place. Cut the wick or string in pieces long enough to form a loop at the top of the ornament for hanging. Dip the ends of the wick in the melted wax and set on wax paper, pushing the ends together to form a loop.

When the wax has melted, stir in the oils and pour the scented wax into the molds using a funnel. Insert the waxed ends of a loop at the top of each mold and place them in a warm place to set. Gently turn the ornaments out when they have hardened.

Ronda Bretz's scented beeswax ornaments lend a tree a delightful old-fashioned feeling while their scent adds to the fragrance of the holidays.

source directory

This source directory lists shops that specialize in herbal products mentioned in this book, the stores where you can buy the supplies to make the items yourself, and the seeds and plants you'd need to grow your own herbs. The code letter (R) after a listing indicates a retail store; (R) (MO), a retail store that sells mail order; (MO), a mail order–only operation. Some may also sell wholesale. Stores vary widely in their hours; it is therefore wise to check by telephone before making a special trip.

CALIFORNIA

AFTON GROVE
1000 Torrey Pines Road
La Jolla, CA 92037
(619) 456-2200
Wreaths, topiaries, potpourris, dried herbs and flowers (R) (MO)

BAY LAUREL FARM
West Garzas Road
Carmel Valley, CA 93924
(408) 659-2913
Rosemary plants, dried herbs and flowers, fresh bay and other wreaths, potpourris (R by appointment) (MO)

DODY LYNESS COMPANY
7336 Berry Hill Drive
Palos Verdes, CA 90274
(213) 377-7040
Wreaths, dried herbs and flowers, potpourri supplies (R) (MO)

HEARD'S COUNTRY GARDENS
14391 Edwards Street
Westminster, CA 92683
(714) 894-2444
Plants, wreaths, arrangements, potpourris (R)

LINDEMANN AG COMPANY
2817 West Locust Avenue
Fresno, CA 93711
(209) 449-1230
Freeze-dried flowers (MO)

JEANNE ROSE
219 Carl Street
San Francisco, CA 94117
(415) 564-6337
Beauty products (R) (MO)

ROSES OF YESTERDAY AND TODAY
802 Brown's Valley Road
Watsonville, CA 95076
(408) 724-3537
Old-fashioned roses (R) (MO)

SAN FRANCISCO HERB COMPANY
250 14th Street
San Francisco, CA 94103
(800) 227-4530
Potpourri, potpourri supplies (MO)

TERRA COTTA
2000 Westridge Road
Los Angeles, CA 90049
(213) 826-7878
Wreaths, topiaries, potpourris, dried arrangements (R) (MO)

CONNECTICUT

CAPRILANDS HERB FARM
Silver Street
Coventry, CT 06238
(203) 742-7244
Seeds, plants, topiaries, wreaths, potpourris, dried herbs and flowers, beauty products (R) (MO)

CATNIP ACRES HERB NURSERY
67 Christian Street
Oxford, CT 06483
(203) 888-5649
Plants, dried herbs and flowers, beauty products, topiaries, potpourris, wreaths (R)

GILBERTIE'S HERB GARDENS
Sylvan Lane
Westport, CT 06880
(203) 227-4175
Plants, topiaries, wreaths, potpourris, beauty products (R)

PARADIS
The River Building
P.O. Box 280
Washington Depot, CT 06794
(203) 868-9401
Dried arrangements, topiaries (R)

PRESERVE THE MEMORIES
102 Westmore Road
Cheshire, CT 06410
(203) 271-1101
Freeze-dried flowers, vegetables (MO)

GEORGIA

JAS KIRKLAND
Kirkland's Woods
Box 533
Swainsboro, GA 31401
(912) 238-3902
Dried flowers, beauty products, potpourris (MO)

IOWA

FRONTIER COOPERATIVE HERBS
Box 299
Norway, IA 52318
(319) 227-7996
Potpourris, potpourri supplies, beauty products (MO)

MAINE

BLACKROCK FARM
Gooserocks Road
Kennebunkport, ME 04014
Mail:
P.O. Box 19
Cape Porpoise, ME 04014
(207) 967-5783
Plants, wreaths, dried arrangements, topiaries (R) (MO except plants)

HEDGEHOG HILL FARM

RFD 2, Box 2010
Buckfield, ME 04220
(207) 388-2341
Dried herbs and flowers, plants, and wreaths
(R) (MO)

MARYLAND

BITTERSWEET HILL NURSERIES

1274 Governor's Bridge Road
Davidsonville, MD 21035
(301) 428-3434
Plants, topiaries (R)

ST. JOHN'S HERB GARDEN, INC.

7711 Hillmeade Road
Bowie, MD 20720
(301) 262-5302
Seeds, plants, dried herbs and flowers, beauty
products, wreaths, potpourris (R) (MO)

STILLRIDGE HERB FARM

10370 Route 99
Woodstock, MD 21163
(301) 465-8348
Plants, seeds, wreaths, potpourris (R) (MO
except plants)

MASSACHUSETTS

CRICKET HILL HERB FARM LTD.

Glen Street
Rowley, MA 01969
(508) 948-2818
Seeds, plants, wreaths, potpourris, dried herbs
and flowers (R) (MO)

HARTMAN'S HERB FARM

Old Dana Road
Barre, MA 01005
(508) 355-2015
Seeds, plants, wreaths, potpourris, dried herbs
and flowers, topiaries (R) (MO)

THE HERB FARM

Barnard Road
Granville, MA 01034
(413) 357-8882
Wreaths, potpourris, dried arrangements (MO)

HERB COUNTRY GIFTS AND COLLECTIBLES

63 Leonard Street
Belmont Center, MA 02178
(508) 263-2405
Plants, wreaths, potpourris, dried herbs and
flowers, beauty products, topiaries (R)

BETSY WILLIAMS/ THE PROPER SEASON

64 Park Street
Andover, MA 01810
(508) 475-2540
Dried herbs and flowers, wreaths, topiaries,
potpourris (R) (MO)

MICHIGAN

FOX HILL FARM

443 West Michigan Avenue
P.O. Box 9
Parma, MI 49269
(517) 531-3179
Plants, topiaries, wreaths (R) (MO)

NEW HAMPSHIRE

APPLE BUTTER HERB FARM

Old Westmoreland Road
Spofford, NH 03462
(603) 363-8902
Plants, wreaths, potpourris (R) (MO)

NEW JERSEY

TOTALLY TOPIARY

Box 191
Stockton, NJ 08559
Topiaries (MO)

WELL-SWEEP HERB FARM

317 Mt. Bethel Road
Port Murray, NJ 07865
(201) 852-5390
Seeds, plants, wreaths, dried herbs and flowers,
potpourris, topiaries (R) (MO)

NEW YORK

APHRODISIA

282 Bleecker Street
New York, NY 10014
(212) 989-6440
Potpourris, dried herbs, beauty products
(R) (MO)

ENGLISH COUNTRY ANTIQUES

Snake Hollow Road
Bridgehampton, NY 11932
(516) 537-0606
Wreaths, arrangements, topiaries, containers
(R) (MO)

FLOWERS FOREVER

311 East 61st Street
New York, NY 10021
(212) 308-0088
Dried herbs and flowers, wreaths, arrangements,
topiaries (R) (MO)

GATEHOUSE HERBS

98 Van Buren Street
Dolgeville, NY 13329
(315) 429-8366
Seeds, plants, dried herbs and flowers, beauty
products, topiaries, wreaths, potpourris (R)
(MO)

EMELIE TOLLEY'S HERB BASKET

Box 1332
Southampton, NY 11969
Wreaths, potpourris, bath herbs (MO)

PINE MEADOW FARM

963 Ripley Lane
Oyster Bay, NY 11771
(516) 626-2735
Wreaths, topiaries, potpourris, dried herbs and
flowers (R) (MO)

SURA KYLA

484 Broome Street
New York, NY
(212) 941-8757
Dried arrangements, topiaries, potpourris (R)

VSF, INC.

204 West 10th Street
New York, NY 10014
(212) 206-7236
Dried herbs and flowers, wreaths, topiaries,
arrangements (R) (MO)

NORTH CAROLINA

GRIFFIN'S

5109 Vickrey Chapel Road
Greensboro, NC 27407
(919) 454-3362
Plants, wreaths, potpourris, topiaries, dried
herbs and flowers (R) (MO except plants)

RASLAND FARM
NC 82 at US 13
Godwin, NC 28344
(919) 567-2705
Plants, dried herbs and flowers, beauty products, topiaries, potpourris, wreaths (R) (MO)

SANDY MUSH HERB NURSERY
Route #2, Surrett Cove Road
Leicester, NC 28748
(704) 683-2014
Plants, seeds, wreaths, topiaries, potpourris (R) (MO)

OHIO

LEWIS MOUNTAIN HERBS AND EVERLASTINGS
2345 State Route 247
Manchester, OH 45144
Plants, wreaths, dried herbs and flowers, topiaries, potpourris, soaps (R) (MO)

WOODSPIRITS SOAPS
1920 Apple Road
St. Paris, OH 43072
(513) 663-4327
Herbal soaps (R) (MO)

OREGON

GOODWIN CREEK GARDENS
154½ Oak Street
Ashland, OR 97520
(503) 488-3308
Plants, seeds, wreaths, potpourris, dried herbs and flowers, topiaries (R) (MO except plants)

HERBFARM
Box 116
Willkins, OR 97544
(206) 784-2222
Plants, seeds, soaps, potpourri, wreaths (R) (MO except plants)

PENNSYLVANIA

ALLOWAY GARDENS AND HERB FARM
456 Mud College Road
Littlestown, PA 17340
(717) 359-4548
Plants, topiaries, wreaths, potpourris, dried flowers and herbs (R) (MO)

DILLWORTHTOWN COUNTRY STORE
275 Burton's Bridge Road
West Chester, PA 19382
(215) 399-0560
Wreaths, garlands, potpourris, dried arrangements, plants, dried flowers (R)

MEADOWBROOK FARM
1633 Washington Lane
Meadowbrook, PA 19046
(215) 887-5900
Plants, topiaries (R)

RHODE ISLAND

COURTYARDS
3980 Main Road
Tiverton, RI 02878
(401) 624-8682
Plants, dried herbs and flowers, beauty products, soaps, wreaths, arrangements (R)

MEADOWBROOK HERB GARDEN
Route 138
Wyoming, RI 02898
(401) 539-7603
Seeds, plants, dried herbs and flowers, topiaries, wreaths, potpourris, beauty products (R) (MO)

TENNESSEE

SASSAFRAS HERBS SHOP
636 Farrell Parkway
P.O. Box 50192
Nashville, TN 37203
(615) 832-2962
Seeds, plants, dried herbs and flowers, beauty products, wreaths, topiaries, potpourris (R) (MO)

TEXAS

FREDERICKSBURG HERB FARM
310 East Main Street
P.O. Drawer 927
Fredericksburg, TX 78624
(512) 997-8615
Wreaths, potpourris, topiaries, beauty products, plants, seeds, dried herbs and flowers (R) (MO except plants)

THE GARDEN SHOP
1832 Bissonet
Houston, TX 77005
(715) 524-1172
Plants, dried herbs and flowers, wreaths, topiaries, potpourris (R)

VERMONT

MEADOWSWEET HERB FARM
Shrewsbury, VT 05738
(802) 492-3566
Plants, seeds, wreaths, potpourris (R) (MO)

SARAH MILEK
Cider Hill Farm
Hunt Road, RR #1, Box 1066
Windsor, VT 05084
(802) 674-5243
Wreaths, dried arrangements (R) (MO)

RATHDOWNEY LTD.
3 River Street
Bethel, VT 05032
(802) 234-9928
Seeds, plants, dried herbs and flowers, beauty products, wreaths, potpourris (R) (MO)

VIRGINIA

T. DEBAGGIO HERBS
923 North Ivy Street
Arlington, VA 22201
(703) 243-2498
Plants, topiaries (R)

TOM THUMB WORKSHOPS
Mappsville, VA 23407
Potpourris, dried herbs and flowers, wreaths (MO)

WASHINGTON

CEDARBROOK HERB FARM
986 Sequim Avenue South
Sequim, WA 98382
(206) 683-7733
Seeds, plants, dried herbs and flowers, wreaths, potpourris (R) (MO)

WISCONSIN

HIDDEN HOLLOW HERBERY
N88 W 8407 Duke Street
Menomonee Falls, WI 53051
Wreaths, potpourris, dried arrangements (R) (MO)